Managing Association Turnarounds

Charles E. Bartling, CAE

The author has worked to ensure that all information in this book is accurate as of the time of publication and consistent with standards of good practice in the general management community. As research and practice advance, however, standards may change. For this reason, it is recommended that readers evaluate the applicability of any recommendation in light of particular situations and changing standards.

Elissa M. Myers, CAE, ASAE Vice President and Publisher
Linda Munday, ASAE Director of Book Publishing

Editor and Production Manager
Marianna Nunan, Gravel Hill Communications, Beltsville, Md.

Designer
Xanthus Design, Washington, D.C.

American Society of Association Executives
1575 I Street, N.W.
Washington, DC 20005
(202) 626-2723
Fax (202) 408-9634
e-mail address: books@asae.asaenet.org

ISBN 0-88034-131-9

Copyright 1997, by the American Society of Association Executives, Washington, D.C.

Permission to reproduce or transmit in any form or by any means, electronic or mechanical, including photocopying and recording, or by an information storage and retrieval system, must be obtained by writing to the director of book publishing or publisher at the address or fax number above.

This book is available at a special discount when ordered in bulk quantities. For information, contact ASAE Member Services at (202) 371-0940.

A complete catalog of titles is available on the ASAE home page at http://www.asaenet.org

TABLE OF CONTENTS

Preface v
Introduction vii
  1. Why Organizations Decline 1
  2. The Early Warnings 9
  3. First Steps 17
  4. Options for Organizational Change 35
  5. Program Options 51
  6. Financial Options 57
  7. Communications Options 69
  8. Characteristics of Turnaround Managers 77
  9. Do Whatever It Takes 79
 10. A Flair for the Dramatic 83
 11. Out-of-the-Box Thinking 87
 12. The Human Factor 91
 13. Operating on Many Fronts 95
 14. Turning Lemons into Lemonade 99
 15. Communications as a Turnaround Tool 103
 16. The Vision Thing 109
 17. Some Personal Thoughts 115
References 119
Appendix A. Sample Plan for the First Eight Weeks 123
Appendix B. The Turnaround Team 133
About the Author 139

Preface

When an organization gets into trouble, it resembles an aircraft tilted downward, with the earth coming up fast. Unless the pilot pulls out of the dive—and soon—the organization perishes, carrying all of its stakeholders with it, including its stockholders (or members, if it is an association), employees, customers, and suppliers—all who depended on it for value added to their lives. In many organizations, the pilot ejects, and a new pilot takes his or her place, with everyone looking to the new hero to stage a dramatic rescue.

This book was conceived as a guide for the pilot, either the one who was in command when the trouble started or the poor soul who was called in after the descent was well under way.

When an organization gets into trouble, it is a time for action—not a time for quiet contemplation about the future of the organization. Unless the right steps are taken immediately, the flight will end in a fiery crash.

This book takes a narrow focus as well. It examines techniques that either have worked or could work for managers of not-for-profit organizations, where funds are limited and the spirit of volunteerism must be tapped.

It is based on personal interviews with scores of managers and consultants, as well as from an extensive review of published material, most of which deals with corporate turnarounds, to determine what similarities exist that can serve as a guide to other managers just beginning to face a power dive within their own organization.

The inspiration for this book came from my experiences as president and chief executive officer of the Financial Institutions Marketing Association (FIMA). FIMA's membership declined sharply during and after the widespread failures that occurred in the nation's savings-and-loan business in the period from 1988 through 1992.

Although FIMA's management took what appeared at the time to be appropriate steps to reduce the overhead of the organization, it never got ahead of the decline in revenues. Consequently, its 30-year build up of reserves was quickly diminished. It was this experience that engendered my quest for practical guidelines for managing an association turnaround.

In a period of decline, the chief staff officer has precious little time available to ponder the reasons for the decline or to carefully craft a plan of action for reversing it. Instead, he or she is constantly involved in putting out small, and sometimes not-so-small, fires to keep the entity alive, while simultaneously crafting a strategy for the rebirth of the organization.

I thought that there surely must be some common elements involved in coping with the sudden decline of a not-for-profit organization, including several techniques that could be borrowed from the for-profit sector, that could serve as a guide for nonprofit managers and their volunteer leaders.

Thanks to funding from the American Society of Association Executives; the nonswerving support of my colleagues at Smith, Bucklin & Associates; the inspiration of a loyal band of dedicated volunteer leaders within the Financial Institutions Marketing Association; and the forbearance of Ann Bartling, my wife, who assumed the role of the household's principal breadwinner during the year-long research and writing period, this book is now a reality.—*Charles E. Bartling, CAE*

INTRODUCTION

Edward J. Collins stepped around the inebriated form of a derelict in a seedy section of Kansas City as he made his way to his new job as president and chief administrative officer of the American Economic Development Association. He had been hired to turn around this association of industrial development executives. His first task was to supervise the move of the association's offices from Kansas City to Schiller Park, Illinois, adjacent to Chicago's O'Hare Airport.

He chatted briefly with his predecessor, who, promptly at 4 p.m., left the office, with the rest of the four-person staff following behind like a column of ducks. Collins was alone, and in one hour the movers were to arrive to empty the offices of its contents and deliver them to Schiller Park.

Rummaging through the desks, he came upon some packages of pressure-sensitive dots in various colors. He went around to each office, applying dots to the furniture and files so he could unravel the mess when it was unloaded into the new offices. Accounting had blue dots; membership was red dots; publications, green dots; and so on.

He was waiting in Illinois when the movers arrived the following week. Before unloading the trucks, they demanded a check for $8,500 to cover the cost of the move. With no checkbook on hand, Collins quickly found a friendly banker who extended the association a line of credit. He discovered later that the association barely had enough assets to cover the loan, much less pay his salary.

From this bleak beginning, he commenced to rebuild the association. Seven years later, in 1988, he left for greener pastures. Reserves had been restored, a small staff was functioning well, and the association was providing its members with a full range of services.

Perhaps one of the most interesting, if frustrating, assignments of an association executive's career is the task of turning around an association under stress. From the interviews with Collins and scores of other association executives, two things stood out:

1. Many association executives have been faced with, or at least perceived they were faced with, a turnaround situation.

2. Very little is published on the subject, except for a few articles in the professional association trade press about individual turnaround cases.

In fact, there are few statistics that quantify the extent to which the association world is faced with problem associations. Anecdotally, however, there is plenty of evidence to support the notion that the need for turnaround management skills is rising.

The restructuring of American business has been a major factor. Daily we read in the newspaper of megamergers of large corporations, usually accompanied with announcements of significant downsizings in the number of workers they employ.

Much of the change in organizations is prompted by the acceptance of the computer in the work place. Initially, the computer simply replaced the typewriter and semiautomated the secretary's job. Later, it reached the executive's desk, and secretaries began to disappear, replaced by an entry-level position known as administrative assistant, which often was a stepping stone to more responsible positions.

Then technology, accompanied by increased competition from other countries, led to a flattening of organization charts and a reengineering of work processes.

All this activity had an impact on the associations that served the affected industries. In my own case, for example, as president and chief executive officer of the Financial Institutions Marketing Association, I witnessed a financial services industry that was shrinking rapidly. Whenever two financial institutions would merge, it seemed, I would get a call from one of my members telling me that his or her marketing department was being consolidated with that of an acquiring company and that the acquired institution's marketing department was being dismantled.

Similarly, of course, new industries and professions have been created, particularly those that deal with evolving technologies. This creates demand for new associations of users of popular software systems, for example, as well as technologically oriented professional societies, such as the Society for Laser Dentistry.

Rapid change creates winners and losers. And it makes life increasingly chaotic for the plodders—those organizations that have settled down into a routine of products and services that are repeated on an annual cycle. As the external environment changes, it inevitably triggers declines in conference registrations and memberships in organizations that have not kept up with these changes.

Stymied by the downward slope, volunteer leaders often take what they perceive as the only way out and replace the chief staff officer. The Search Committee reaches down into the middle management level of successful associations to anoint a new chief executive, who faces a massive turnaround situation—ready or not. Complicating the matter is the fact that the association is operating without a CEO for six months or longer during the search process, and the deterioration of the association accelerates during that period.

Hence, as was the case with Ed Collins, a turnaround often is the first management challenge to be tackled by a new association CEO, who generally is unprepared by training and experience to deal with it successfully. In fact, many association executives are unaware of the need for turnaround management until after their first days or weeks on the job. Even those with advanced degrees in management are faced with an absence of role models to emulate, because the emphasis in business schools since World War II has been on the challenges of managing unbridled growth, not on dealing with business declines. This book is intended to provide some guidance to those new association CEOs, as well as to serve as a wakeup call for experienced executives who may be settling into a management rut. It also should be instructive to volunteer leaders who are stymied by an association or society that appears to be in a funk.

One basic premise is that, when one examines the actions taken in a successful turnaround, patterns will appear. Certain techniques work time after time. Certain mistakes are commonly made and dealt with in ways that have similar results. Of course, association management is an art, not a science, and a cookie-cutter approach will not work. But there is something to be said for learning from experience, and it is from that assumption that I have entered into this project.

My approach was to interview executives who engineered successful turnarounds and to discover those patterns that commonly produced predictable results that can be assimilated by other association executives. The research was not limited to the not-for-profit world. The practices of for-profit companies also were examined to extract those techniques that could be replicated in the not-for-profit world.

Differences Between For-Profits and Not-for-Profits

A reasonable assumption is that the for-profit environment is somewhat different from the not-for-profit sector because of differences in ownership and governance.

Ownership in the for-profit world is largely of an absentee nature, by investors who are looking primarily for a financial return on their investment. In the not-for-profit sector, by contrast, the "owners," or members, are typically the organization's customers and are more interested in the products of the organization than they are in the financial results.

Governing boards of for-profit entities often are representative of the major stockholders, yet they typically are hand-picked by the chief executive officer and rarely will second-guess his or her decisions unless they have serious legal or financial ramifications.

For example, Rutgers professor, economist, and banking consultant Paul Nadler noted in an article he wrote for the *American Banker* (26 September 1995) newspaper that most bank directors fall into one of three categories:

- "Inside directors, whose backbones are made of jelly because the CEO sets their salary and ultimately decides whether they get to keep their jobs...."
- "Celebrities, who do nothing but look good. They don't want to endanger their sinecures by rocking the boat."
- "People with close connections to the CEO—either friends or lawyers, accountants, or others whose fees from the bank depend on staying in the boss' good graces...."

Or, as *Business Week* (25 November 1996) put it in a special report on corporate boards: "After all, shareholders don't give a hoot how often a board meets, how glittering the resumes of its members are, or what probing questions they ask the CEO. What matters is how much money the company returns to shareholders."

Governing boards in the not-for-profit sector, on the other hand, usually are selected by a nominating committee of members who may or may not owe allegiance to the chief staff officer. While they naturally are concerned with the financial health of the organization, they receive no financial dividends, nor are they pressured by members to produce a financial return. Consequently, they typically are more concerned with the nature of the association's program and the quality of the service than they are with profits generated by those activities. They typically view the chief staff officer as one of their employees, rather than as their benefactor.

The for-profit executive must constantly keep one eye open for attempted raids on his or her organization by outside investors, while keeping the other eye on the price of the company's stock in the marketplace. The not-for-profit executive is concerned primarily with satisfying his or her board, while simultaneously developing and managing a program that meets the needs of the membership and supports the mission of the organization, all the while operating the association as a business to maintain its financial viability.

Interviews revealed that in some instances, association executives take a dictatorial stance with their board. Their message is essentially: "You are in bad shape, but I can get you out of it. It will take quick action and snap decisions. Therefore, I want you to delegate to me the authority to take whatever action seems necessary at the time. I will keep you thoroughly informed about the actions I take, but I will not ask you for permission in advance."

Most executives find such an approach to be fraught with danger. The more typical attitude can be summed up this way: "You are in trouble, but together we will work our way out of it. I will help you articulate a vision for the association, and I will offer alternative courses of action, based on our actual and potential resources. The journey will not necessarily be a pleasant one. Some formerly sacred cows will be gored in the process. Upon taking your vision into consideration, I will present a plan for your review and acceptance that will bring us, step by step, out of the abyss we're in. At all times, you will be in control, but together, in an atmosphere of mutual respect, we will make this thing work."

Also, one should not discount the value of "in-kind" assistance from volunteers that uniquely benefits not-for-profits. This was dramatically brought home to me in 1995, when I assumed the presidency of a club affiliated with Toastmasters International. This particular club was a company club, which means that all of its members were employed by the same company.

At the first meeting of the club's officers, I invited my predecessor to report on the year just concluded. He announced that during his tenure, there were no cash withdrawals from the club's treasury. Imagine that? Here was a not-for-profit organization that held regular meetings and functioned normally for an entire year without spending any money!

The company provided one of its conference rooms for the meetings at no charge. Speakers reproduced their own handouts for distribution to members. Communication with members and prospective members was conducted entirely by telephone and by messages on the company's electronic mail system. Even though modest dues were assessed and the club treasury amounted to several hundreds of dollars, there just did not happen to be an occasion during that year to spend any of the club's funds.

Such an experience is virtually unheard-of in the for-profit sector, where a healthy bottom line is assumed to be the primary reason for the company's existence. In the not-for-profit sector, on the other hand, the "mission" is the important thing, and it is rarely expressed in terms of dollars. If the organization's mission is considered by its members to be worthwhile, whether it is to find a cure for a rare disease, to make the world safer for a specific industry, or to provide an essential educational component to members with a common interest, it is theoretically possible for that organization to exist entirely on time and resources supplied at no charge by its members.

Thus, the not-for-profit turnaround specialist possesses the ultimate weapon of turning the financial spigot all the way to off, if sufficient in-kind services are made available by a dedicated core of members. Such an alternative is rarely, if ever, available in the for-profit world.

Dr. Philip Lesser, Ph.D., CAE, a past president of the Chicago Society of Association Executives and a vice president of the Bostrom Corporation, says it well when he notes that "associations have a tremendous advantage over profit-making companies because our members are members; they are not just customers. Members have a sense of affiliation and affinity to the association that customers don't."

When the National School Public Relations Association (NSPRA) was in deep financial trouble, for example, a group of past presidents met informally by telephone conference call and collectively asked its new executive director, Richard Bagin, who had been hired to attempt a turnaround, if there was anything they could do to help. He suggested developing a workshop that featured the association's past presidents as speakers. It was billed as "the finest minds in school PR." The workshop was a financial success and was cited by Bagin as a significant factor in that organization's turnaround.

Of course, many association executives will counter that their members are acting more and more like customers every day, but nonetheless, the "member" mind-set is decidedly different from either the "customer" or the "stockholder" mind-set. And in a turnaround, that can make a big difference.

The NSPRA experience demonstrates the power of another valuable resource readily available to association executives that is not as available in the for-profit sector. Glen Anderson, an account executive with Smith, Bucklin, and Associates, Inc., calls it the "professional brain trust." Each industry or profession has individuals who are widely regarded as the leading-edge "thinkers" about the industry. Many are former board members and officers, some are consultants, others are from academia. These individuals are frequently called on to speak at industry seminars and conferences, and they often are published authors in journals read by members.

Successful association turnaround executives are in regular communication with this "brain trust" through letters, telephone calls, and now, more frequently, through electronic mail. Because of the competitive nature of business, few for-profit executives enjoy the access to a top-level brain trust of industry leaders as that enjoyed by association executives, Anderson contends.

In a turnaround situation, the association's best and brightest members can be a valuable resource in obtaining a "quick read" about the merits of potential strategies and tactics.

Characteristics of Successful Turnaround Managers

Both in the literature and in the interviews, a frequent observation was that turnaround managers are somehow different than their "maintenance" brethren in that the skills of one are not necessarily the skills of the other. Consequently a turnaround artist is often "used up" and replaced by a different executive after stability has been obtained.

The turnaround manager is, above all, a change agent. He or she must be strong-willed, decisive, goal-oriented, multifaceted, entrepreneurial, innovative, and willing and able to turn on a dime. The maintenance manager, on the other hand, needs to be a planner, consensus-builder, long-range thinker, and a detail-oriented administrator.

The ideal manager, of course, would have all these attributes. But in the real world, few individuals do, and that's why executive leaders often are divided into two camps—the fixers and the builders. In a turnaround, the fixers have the upper hand. But it's like fixing a house while you're living in it. All the while that walls are being torn down and collapsed structures are being rebuilt, the life of the family must continue. Similarly, an association must satisfy the here-and-now demands of its members even as it charts a new future.

How they do it is through a combination of panache, enthusiasm, cajoling, humor, creativity, chutzpah, and plain old hard work. Chapter 1 begins the fascinating journey through the world of turnaround management for associations.

1 | WHY ORGANIZATIONS DECLINE

The human condition welcomes stability and routine. We would like nothing better than to find the formula for success in our association and to apply that formula on a regular and consistent basis. "If it ain't broke, don't fix it" is a maxim that most executives would like to subscribe to, even as life in the nineties has made a mockery of the phrase. As conditions change, we tend to look on those changes as aberrations and tell ourselves that, after we straighten things out, life will return to normal, and we can enjoy managing our associations again.

During much of the post-World War II era, growth was the key ingredient in change. Executives gained power and promotion as their empires grew. It was a mark of achievement to expand the workforce under your command, whether it was a division of a large entity or the entire organization itself. Pay raises often were based on growth of the executive's budget and payroll.

Turnaround management was a skill that rarely, if ever, was needed by the typical executive. Declining sales were, more often than not, caused by a failure to promote aggressively. The prescription was invariably a better designed brochure mailed out to a larger mailing list, and sales would rebound.

During the 1980s, it became apparent that the post-World War II boom was nearing an end, and overseas competitors began making serious inroads into U.S. markets. The Japanese, in particular, proved to be aggressive competitors who put a premium on product and service quality. Meanwhile, bloated payrolls at many U.S. companies were escalating costs to noncompetitive levels. As the decade of the 1990s began, "downsizing" and "reengineering" became popular words in the management lexicon.

Another factor that added to the turmoil was the rapid pace of technological change. When the Russians launched Sputnik into the skies in the 1950s, America responded by increasing the emphasis on science in the classroom. Engineering became a popular course of study. Then when President Kennedy in the 1960s established the goal of putting a man on the moon by the end of that decade, technological research escalated to a feverish pitch.

Typically, associations mirror the constituencies they serve. If downsizing, reengineering, and technological change are prevalent in a given industry, the associations that serve that industry are expected by the volunteer leadership to engage in similar downsizing, reengineering, and technological upgrading activities. Likewise, as turnaround management became the growth industry of the nineties in the corporate world, it also became a growth industry in the not-for-profit world.

Just as rapid change has become a hallmark of virtually every segment of human activity, so has change become a constant with associations. Consequently, it behooves association executives to be constantly aware of changes that may affect their associations. The ability to project how those changes will affect their associations is rapidly becoming a critical management skill for association executives.

The changes that cause an association to head into a downward spiral are of two types: external and internal. The collapse of the savings-and-loan industry in 1989-90, for example, was an external event that sent the Financial Institutions Marketing Association into sudden and traumatic decline, because more than 80 percent of its members were employed by the industry.

The Fibre Box Association was similarly affected when a significant antitrust action, alleging price fixing, was leveled by the federal government against many of the major firms in the industry following World War II. Significant and prolonged earnings declines in an industry, from whatever cause, can be counted on to have a negative impact on the associations serving that industry.

In fact, expenditures for activities conducted by trade associations and professional societies are an easy target when a company's earnings are challenged. Membership and participation in an association results in long-term benefits, while the expenditures required are of an immediate nature. Therefore, when push comes to shove, company executives find they can jump-start their company's earnings by slashing expenditures for membership dues and attendance at conferences and seminars—both mainstays of the typical association's revenue stream.

Competitive changes represent another external category of decline. Competition affecting the members of an association is one thing, but associations also must be conscious of competition with respect to their services and activities. Nonassociation trade publications, for example, have become quite aggressive in sponsoring trade shows and conferences that cut into the nondues income of associations in their field. Suppliers to an industry also will organize user groups that compete directly with associations in the areas of information and education.

Turnaround Tip No. 1

"Mergers are increasingly representing the strategic direction of most associations. You must decide whether you are going to be an acquirer or an acquiree."

—**Glen R. Anderson**

Account Executive, Smith, Bucklin & Associates, Inc.

Competition often is aided and abetted by technological changes. In 1995 and 1996, for example, thousands of new information sources suddenly became accessible on that unofficial worldwide linkup of computers known as the Internet. Whether looking for a recipe for lamb chops or a source for used toilet tank lids, millions of Americans found they could turn to their computers to get instant answers to arcane questions.

Companies, associations, and individuals alike found that they could inexpensively create home pages on a segment of the Internet known as the World Wide Web that could provide answers to all kinds of questions. And the kind of networking that traditionally occurs within the confines of an association became routine on thousands of Internet-connected bulletin boards and special-interest discussion groups.

In fact, some virtual associations have been created in this technological Twilight Zone that function without a paid staff or physical headquarters. Over the next few years, such technological changes could exert a dramatic impact on the way associations are organized and managed, in much the same way that television drastically altered the structure and content of the radio and motion picture industries, among others.

Vast communications conglomerates are being created through mergers of companies in the television, computer, and telephone industries that have created the expectation that big changes in the movement of information and commerce will occur before the end of the decade/century/millennium. There is no doubt that associations will be affected significantly by these changes.

In the meantime, a revolution is occurring in government and politics, involving the basic philosophy of the mission of the national government and the interrelationships between Washington and the individual states. Layered on top of this activity is a growing globalization of business and industry that threatens to vault government changes to the top of the categories of concerns facing the management of associations.

Societal changes is another category that must be monitored by associations. The aging of the Baby Boom generation, in particular, is affected by and is having a causative effect on some of the other types of changes mentioned here, ranging from the Social Security safety net to the delivery of health care to the elderly.

Economic, competitive, technological, governmental, and social changes, therefore, all constitute a menu of challenges that will shape, distort, and cause sleepless nights for many an association executive concerned about the relevance, existence, and growth of his or her association.

Internal Causes

If the external environment of the association is favorable, yet the association itself is foundering, then the cause of the decline is likely to be internal. This is a good-news-bad-news situation. It's good news because the turnaround manager has the opportunity to do something about it. But it's bad news in that the turnaround strategy can be easily botched.

The critical element is in determining whether the cause is operational or strategic, and therein lies the trap. Turnaround consultants note that the cause of organizational decline is most often strategic, but the remedies most often employed are operational.

On this matter, volunteer leaders often will lead the executive astray. They typically have their strategic blinders on and invariably will insist that their problems can be cured by operational efficiencies. If we just redesign the logo, add four-color art to the magazine, and ask each board member to send out new-member brochures to his or her professional network, then all our troubles will be over, they contend. More often than not, the mix of association programs is failing to provide solutions to members' problems.

Veteran association executive Mary Jane Kolar, CAE, who

heads her own association management firm, notes that boards of directors frequently can be a part of the problem in a turnaround because they are not representative of the membership as a whole. They tend to be much more sophisticated and experienced than the rank-and-file member and consequently often are unaware of the needs of the vast majority of regular members.

She notes that those associations with a strategic plan, or where the board is committed to the strategic planning process, are much better candidates for a successful turnaround than those that have no strategic plan.

"The most successful turnarounds," she contends, "are the ones where the (chief elected officer) knows how to be a leader and forms a partnership with the board. And where the chairman and the board know how to mobilize the membership."

By definition, an operational problem is characterized by inefficiencies in the operation. A strategic problem, on the other hand, is one in which the association is not meeting the needs of its members; that is, it is attempting to do the wrong things, even though they may be well-executed.

Fixing operational problems is relatively easy, because there are only three basic operational turnaround strategies: cost-cutting, revenue-generating, and asset reduction. But strategic problems are tougher to identify and to deal with, because they suggest that the association is not doing the right things. It may be doing everything right, but if it's doing the wrong things, then all is for naught.

Operational problems require a capable and dedicated staff. But in a turnaround situation, staff often are demoralized, because they perceive (quite accurately in many cases) that their jobs are at stake, particularly when the financial situation is deteriorating rapidly.

While the executives interviewed spoke in some cases of yeomen's service, nearing heroic proportions, on the part of many a beleaguered staff, the stories are matched by others that tell of fictionalized membership statistics and outright plundering of the association treasury, exhibiting an attitude of "I'd better get mine before the well runs dry" on the part of some staffers.

Membership records, in particular, are easy to manipulate and are almost never subjected to an independent audit, as financial records are. Consequently, it is not unusual for a newly hired executive to discover that what she thought was a 2,000-member organization consisted of only 800 who were current in their dues. The rest had died, were retired, had left the profession, or had elected not to renew their membership, yet they were still carried on the membership rolls, sometimes for years.

Corporate turnaround specialist Donald B. Bibeault contends that "in practice, most firms that have failed in their turnaround attempts have usually tried an operational turnaround when in fact a strategic turnaround plan was called for."

A firm in a strong strategic position that is in average operating health, he says, is seldom in need of a turnaround. "When a business is strong operationally but weak strategically," he warns, "strategic turnaround is indicated but usually not attempted."

Whether the problem is external or internal, strategic or operational, the situation often is exacerbated when an angry elected leadership summarily terminates the chief staff officer. It then embarks on a search for a new CEO that can take upwards of six to nine months. In the meantime, a weakening association, with no executive leadership, continues to decline, at an accelerated pace.

How can we tell when a turnaround strategy is imminent? The early warning signs are explored in Chapter 2.

Turnaround Tip No. 2

"Get a couple of allies on the board that you can work with. Use them as a resource. Don't go off and think that you can do it yourself. People will respect you if you ask them for advice."

—**Jonathan Perman**

Executive Director, Evanston (Ill.) Chamber of Commerce

2 | The Early Warnings

A meteorologist can tell by looking at a barometer that conditions are changing and that a storm is brewing, even before the wind picks up or the clouds begin to gather. Similarly, there is a barometer for association executives that foretells trouble ahead. That barometer is the membership list, both the raw number of members and the segmentation of those numbers. A skillful and consistent reading of those numbers can be revealing.

There are many ways to segment the membership, depending on your association. At the Financial Institutions Marketing Association, for example, members came from four distinct industry segments: commercial banks, credit unions, savings institutions, and service firms.

The first three categories could be further broken down by asset size—those with assets of less than $100 million, assets of $100 million to $1 billion, and assets greater than $1 billion. Other industries may find sales or number of outlets to be significant segment identifiers. Or it might be geography, household income, age, sex, or educational degrees.

The numbers continually change for two reasons: (1) new members come in and (2) old members drop out. A consistent charting of the new-member experience and the old-member renewal rate can provide management with a constant reading of the present and future health of the organization.

If membership begins to decline, and the staff or volunteers responsible for drafting the budget insert realistic budget numbers that assume a continued decline, that is certainly an early warning sign, because the association is literally budgeting itself out of existence unless it has a plan for reversing the decline.

Financial results, of course, are another place to look for trouble signs. In good years, a not-for-profit organization actually makes a profit on its operations and puts those profits into its reserve fund. This fund sustains the operation in poor years, when income fails to match expenses. It also finances forays into new services, which may operate at a loss for awhile before paying their own way or contributing to reserves. Some services, such as maintenance of an industry library, lobbying activities, and the collection of industry statistics, will never generate a profit.

Keep in mind, however, that not-for-profit organizations exist primarily to perform services that are not feasible in the for-profit sector. Therefore, it is not uncommon for them to operate some or all of their programs at a loss. This operating deficit is overcome by collecting taxes in the case of governmental institutions; by soliciting contributions in the case of charitable, educational, and religious organizations; or by assessing dues in the case of most trade associations and professional societies. Nevertheless, over the long term, it is essential that all organizations—even the federal government—operate on at least a break-even basis financially.

If the association registers back-to-back years of deficits, requiring it to tap into its reserves, then it merits a closer look to determine why those deficits were incurred and to take steps to reverse the decline in those reserve funds.

A third sign of trouble is declining participation in measurable, on-going events, such as the annual convention. If attendance at the annual meeting is on a downward slope, it may signal that the pool of members is shrinking or that the association is becoming less relevant to its members. Likewise, if book sales decline, if fewer members respond to membership surveys, or if entries in the annual awards competition begin to trail off, then these may constitute possible warning signs.

It's important to determine the reasons for the decline in participation. Too often, there's a tendency to blame the promotional efforts, such as the graphic design of the brochure, the quality of the mailing list, or the lack of an effective telemarketing campaign. More likely, the real reasons for the decline are of a strategic nature—that the program or programs are no longer meeting the needs of the membership.

Although member erosion, financial deficits, and a decline in program participation are the primary signs of trouble, there are other indications as well. These include a shrinkage of the industry served by the association, resignations by staff and board members, or evidence that other associations in the industry are thriving at a time when your association is experiencing difficulties.

Association leaders, particularly board members and officers whose terms will be ending in the next one to three years, tend to overlook these early warning signs. Therefore, denial is a constant enemy to early actions that may avert a crisis.

Turnaround specialist A. David Silver, author of *When the Bottom Drops* (1988), contends that survival requires an organization's leaders to avoid denial. "If you feel uncertain about the economy, your region, your industry, or the efficacy of your company's technology," he writes, "then you are experiencing a stressor event. Deny the signals, and you are dead. Treat the murmurs and whispers with a 'no problem' disdain, and you are dead. Go to fancy power breakfasts with those who would idolize you when you should be crisis-formulating, and you are dead."

"Just remember: No business ever failed because it was overprepared. An active denial system prolongs and deepens a crisis. It delays implementing the plans that could save the company."

Reexamine the Mission

Perhaps the most insidious cause of decline is the gradual erosion of the association's very reason for existence. It is characterized by the boiled frog syndrome.

Researchers found that if you take a frog from a room-temperature environment and throw it into a pot of hot water, it will immediately sense the danger and will hop out. But if you put the frog into water at room temperature and gradually heat it up, by the time the frog realizes it is in trouble, it is too late to jump, and it will boil to death.

> **Turnaround Tip No. 3**
>
> "There's nothing more dangerous than a past president with a current member list."
>
> —Rodney S. Brutlag, CAE
>
> President, Brutlag & Associates, Inc.

Similarly, organizations will head into decline, even though they have done everything right from an operational point of view. An example is the National Association of Bank Women. Established in 1921, when few financial institutions employed women as officers, the organization initially served as a refuge for female bankers, who met regularly in local groups to exchange information and ideas on how to succeed in a male-dominated industry. Then in the 1970s and 1980s, the organization grew spectacularly, reaching 28,000 members by 1985, as pressures for affirmative action increased and some of the barriers against female bank officers seemed to be dropping.

But the very success of the organization in fulfilling its mission contributed to a substantial decline in members during the 1990s, as women became assimilated into the mainstream of banking. By the mid-1990s, membership had declined to fewer than 10,000, as mergers and acquisitions rapidly depleted the financial services workforce and further aggravated the decline.

The association, subsequently renamed Financial Women International (FWI), was still providing an excellent opportunity for women in financial services to network with each other and to discuss how to break the industry's glass ceiling, while some of the very problems they were railing against were becoming less and less relevant. Women were becoming assimilated into the banking culture at a fairly rapid pace, and the new women leaders were seeking leadership opportunities in organizations that formerly were bastions of male dominance.

In other words, the relevancy of the organization was being eroded, even as the association's programs were being executed well.

Fortunately, the organization's leaders took strong action in the mid-1990s to reinvent the association from a strategic point of view. It widened its membership to include other sectors of the industry and made a determined effort to attract members from countries outside the United States. It also refocussed its efforts on workforce issues that were becoming more important to its constituencies, as the complexities and pressures of work lives increased. By 1997, the association had stabilized its membership, and its staff and volunteer leaders were working cooperatively to rebuild the organization.

To continue the boiled frog metaphor, FWI is an organization that has turned the burner down sufficiently far enough in advance to give the frog a nice warm bath, rather than boiling it to death.

Another example of the boiled frog syndrome was the Bank Marketing Association, organized in 1915 as the Financial Advertisers Association. For years, the organization operated as a refuge for financial marketers, who generally were unappreciated in their highly regulated industry.

But as marketing became more widely accepted as a

discipline that was important to the success of banking organizations, the need for the organization began to erode. In this case, the frog did hop out of the water. The organization became an affiliate of the American Bankers Association and continued to exist as the information and educational arm of marketing in banking, with a mission that still retained its relevancy.

The concept of strategic drift is a difficult one for association boards of directors to comprehend, let alone to deal with. For the most part, board members have attained their positions within the association because of their strong commitment to its ideals, and they resent any suggestion that the organization may be losing its relevancy.

As one executive director confessed to his volunteer leaders, "Sometimes I wake up in the middle of the night and ask myself if there really is a need for this organization." He was immediately taken to task by the elected officers for this remark and was accused of a lack of commitment to the organization.

Peter F. Drucker, professor of social sciences at the Claremont Graduate School in California, contends that neither layoffs nor reengineering is likely to restore an ailing company to health. "A company beset by malaise and steady deterioration," he wrote in the *Wall Street Journal* (2 February 1993), "suffers from something far more serious than inefficiencies. Its 'business theory' has become obsolete."

"Whenever a business keeps on going downhill despite massive spending and heroic efforts by its people," he wrote, "the most likely cause is the obsolescence of its business theory. This diagnosis becomes a virtual certainty if (a) the malaise follows long years of unbroken success, or if (b) newcomers to the industry flourish while the long-time leaders are fading."

He cited as an example that Wal-Mart was prospering while Sears was in decline. "To start the turnaround," he advised, "thus requires a willingness to rethink and to re-examine the company's business theory. It requires stopping saying 'we know' and instead saying 'let's ask.' And there are two sets of questions that need to be asked. First: Who are the customers and who are the noncustomers? What is value to them? What do they pay for? Second: What do the successes—the Wal-Marts, the regional banks, and so on—do that we do not do? What do they not do that we know is essential? What do they assume that we know to be wrong?"

It is difficult for the managers who made the mistakes to admit they were wrong, Drucker noted, which is why turnarounds are seldom implemented until new management comes on the scene.

"Re-examining an ailing company's business theory," Drucker maintained, "almost always shows right away that the best resources are misinvested. People, knowledge, money are committed to things that should be stopped or sharply curtailed. Some of these will be things that should be done—but by other people and by another company. Other things have outlived their validity and productivity. Yet others should never have been done at all—typically, things into which the company rushed in reaction to malaise and decline. Getting rid of these things will not, by itself, generate new growth. But unless they are gotten out of the way, the company will have neither the vision nor the energy nor the resources to do the right things, the things that will produce results and growth."

With rapid changes in the years ahead, existing theories of the business will increasingly—and in an accelerating manner—become obsolete, in Drucker's view. "In fact," he asserted, "the most probable assumption is that no currently working business theory will be valid 10 years hence—at least not without major modifications."

Thus, a critical challenge to an association's managers and directors is to take a penetrating look at the organization's business theory, to ask itself the following question: *If this association did not exist, would we sacrifice considerable time and money to create it? And if we did, how would it differ from the organization that exists today?*

3 First Steps

An organization in decline often goes through a period of denial. During this period, management and the volunteer leadership may insist that conditions will change for the better, if they just tough it out. Such an attitude can be dangerous. In today's fast-changing world, conditions seldom revert to those of the good old days. They may get better, but when they do, chances are they will be different.

Corporate turnaround specialist Donald B. Bibeault contends in *Corporate Turnaround—How Managers Turn Losers into Winners* (1982) that there are five stages to successful turnarounds:

1. Management change
2. Evaluation
3. Emergency
4. Stabilization
5. Return to normal growth

The techniques for managing a turnaround are different from the techniques for managing in a more positive environment. Consequently, volunteer leaders may call for a new CEO who is not hampered by attempts to justify past decisions. On the other hand, some successful turnarounds have been conducted by existing management.

More often than not, a personnel change is dictated by the circumstances of the turnaround. If current management comes to the board and declares that the ship is sinking and that it wishes to employ radical new strategies to fix it, the board is more likely to give present managers a chance.

But if the pressure for change comes from the volunteer leaders, they are more likely to demand that a new chief staff executive be hired to engineer the change. Nevertheless, whether existing management is retained or new management hired, a decision must be made to change the way the association is being managed. Before new strategies can be suggested, the organization's leaders must agree on the causes of their present predicament. Otherwise, the wrong strategies will be attempted.

> **Turnaround Tip No. 4**
>
> "No matter how bad it is, it's always going to be worse."
>
> —**David M. Patt, CAE**
>
> Executive Director, Chicago Area Runners Association

External Factors

When the problems are external, the solutions can be extremely daunting. It is unlikely that changes in the association will rescue a profession or an industry that is shrinking because of economic conditions, technology, societal changes, competitive pressures, or government imperatives. If those are the causes of decline, then the association may need either to find a new market for its services or to seek a merger partner.

A creative solution to a declining industry was implemented by the Iowa League of Savings Institutions. At its peak, in the 1940s, the association consisted of 119 members, primarily savings and loan associations in the state of Iowa. The following year, disaster struck the savings and loan business nationally, resulting in hundreds of institutional failures throughout the country, with Iowa suffering its share.

As the industry dug out from its troubles, a general restructuring of the financial services industry resulted in many of the association's members going out of business, merging with each other, or being acquired by commercial banks. When the leaders of the Iowa League convened for a strategic planning session in 1987, they estimated that within a few years, the number of members would drop into the teens.

Most groups would consider such a turn of events to be an invitation to dissolution, but not the Iowa League. Thanks to quick thinking on the part of its chief staff officer, Richard L. Goodson, the league formed a for-profit subsidiary, Diversified Management Services (DMS), to function as an association management company.

Initially, the League became a client of its subsidiary, while the staff went out and beat the bushes for additional clients. As this is written, DMS manages 11 groups, ranging from the Society of Iowa Florists and Growers to the National Association for Family Child Care.

Gradually, the League sold off stock in the subsidiary to the subsidiary's employees. Then in 1995, according to Goodson, the League's Executive Committee decided it should get out of the association management business, and the League sold the rest of its interest to the management company's employees.

So even though the League's membership had declined substantially in line with its industry, the association flourished as never before. When the subsidiary was established in 1988, it had six employees. Eight years later, the for-profit Diversified Management Services boasted a payroll of seventeen.

"To top it all off," Goodson says, "the League's members feel they are getting just as good service today as they were getting when they had a standalone staff."

Internal Factors

In many cases, the cause of decline is internal, rather than external. If the industry is flourishing while the association is languishing, then it is likely that the cause is an internal one. The association may need to change the way it is organized and managed. Of course, it is possible that the causes might involve both external and internal factors.

Stages of a Successful Turnaround

The emergency stage is characterized by steps taken to stop the bleeding. If the organization is operating at a deficit, gradually (or perhaps not-so-gradually) eroding the association's fund balance, then emergency steps need to be taken quickly to preserve capital for rebuilding the association. The next chapter covers specific options associations have taken to deal with such a situation.

If the association is successful at stemming the bleeding, it then enters the stabilization stage, where the cash flow becomes more manageable. Stabilization is characterized as a period when revenues equal or exceed expenses. It is much like being in the eye of a hurricane. For the time being, the seas are smooth, but unless further steps are taken, the ship could easily be overwhelmed by a sudden squall.

It is at this point that the emphasis shifts from cash flow and survival to rebuilding and reposturing. It is particularly important in the stabilization stage to pay attention to the core services of the association, because the excess revenues they generate will ultimately provide the capital for investment in new programs and services that will help the association move forward.

The final stage constitutes the return to normal growth. Here, the association board reestablishes its vision for the future and charts a strategy for building the membership and directing the program to achieve the vision.

In a turnaround, time is of the essence. The sooner you make the circuit from the first stage to the last stage, the better, because the world keeps changing at a dizzying pace. Let's see how that might be accomplished in an association setting.

Finding and Analyzing the Facts

The first step in a turnaround is to gather the facts and to analyze those facts thoroughly and quickly. Otherwise, you may be solving the wrong problems and not working on the critical issues. Before you begin, Mary Jane Kolar, CAE, recommends that you schedule a board meeting about 60 days into the future and promise the board you will present an interim plan of action at that time. Making that commitment will provide an added incentive to get it done, both for them and for you.

In an association, the financial and membership records are a good place for you to begin your fact-finding mission. Ideally you should have a balance sheet and income statement that have been audited by an independent outside auditing firm.

Most large associations and many well-run small associations will have had their financial statements reviewed through an outside audit. But many of the turnaround executives interviewed only had a financial statement that the previous executive drafted that had no standing in the real world.

You need to verify the assets. Don't accept someone's word that the checking account has $10,000 in it. Check the latest bank statement, and look at the association's checkbook. One should support the other. Question any item on the balance sheet or the income statement that you don't understand.

Determine your contractual commitments, especially hotel contracts for future meetings. It is not unusual for the annual meeting to be booked for several years in advance, with substantial penalties for cancellation or modification, particularly within a year of the meeting. If the association has been declining for some time, then the attendance estimates for next

> **Turnaround Tip No. 5**
>
> "Understand the culture. Develop the core values and stick to them. Contrary to conventional wisdom, learn what works and don't change things just because it's fashionable to change them. Remember the past."
>
> —J.C. (Chris) Mahaffey, CAE
>
> Executive Director, Chicago Society of Association Executives

year's convention might have been stated in the contract at unrealistically high levels.

Ask about office and equipment leases, pension plan liabilities (including promises made to retirees), and publication contracts. Is there a company-owned automobile? Have payroll taxes been paid to federal, state, and local governments?

Sometimes, arrangements that associations have made with outside entities can be substantial. Donald E. Manger discovered, for example, that 20 percent of the Treasury Management Association's annual revenues were spent with an independent contractor that produced communications materials for the association.

Are the financial records stated on a cash basis or an accrual basis? If you don't understand that question, you should get an accountant on the case right away. Many associations that are alive today on a cash basis are theoretically bankrupt because they are using next year's dues or conference fees to pay this year's bills.

Financial statements should be produced and distributed to the entire board of directors at least monthly. If they have not been, then tell your bookkeeper that from now on, you want to see a statement each month. Also tell the bookkeeper that you want to see a copy of each deposit slip and that you will personally sign each check, which should be accompanied by the proper documentation.

Ask about the procedure for depositing checks. The person who makes the deposit should not be the same one who opens the mail and records the receipts. Also ask about disbursement procedures. The person authorizing and signing checks should not be the same person who prepares the checks and records them in the general ledger.

In some cases, the new executive director will take a direct, hands-on approach to gain a full comprehension of the depths of the association's financial problems. When G. Martin Moelle Jr., assumed command of the Washington Chapter of the

American Institute of Architects in 1990, for example, he found that the bookkeeping of the $300,000 annual budget organization was in disarray, and much of it had been outsourced.

"I brought all basic bookkeeping functions in-house and personally wrote out the checks, signed them with the treasurer, and monitored every deposit," he said, "so that I knew about every penny that was coming in or going out. That was vital for me to begin to trace what the problems were and then to establish the controls needed from an accounting standpoint." Although an outside accountant was retained to review the books and prepare the monthly operating statements for the board, Moeller actually maintained this level of control for about two years.

Spend a full day with your membership director. Take a look at the most recent membership statement and ask the director how he or she arrived at each number on that statement. Break down the membership by the amount of dues paid. Suppose the director tells you that the association has 1,500 members, including 1,000 regular members who pay $100 a year in dues and 500 associate members who pay $50 a year each.

Do the math. The 1,000 regular members should bring in $100,000, and the 500 associate members should yield $25,000. Then check the income statement for the past year and add up the total income received from dues. If the number doesn't approximate $125,000, find out why it does not.

Generate a list of those 1,500 members in alphabetical order. Scan the list and question whether C. Edward Brown and Charles E. Brown, who are both vice presidents at the Schmidlap National Bank, might be the same person. Pick out a name at random and ask to see that person's record on the computer. Then ask your membership director to show you the field on the computer screen that tells when that person paid his or her dues and how much was paid.

Find out how a record is created, how a record is deleted,

and how data are changed. Have the director show you the procedure that's followed when a dues check comes into the office. In other words, "get your hands dirty with the data."

One executive, who for obvious reasons shall remain anonymous, told me that "every time I opened up a filing cabinet, the bones rattled and the ghosts appeared. The first thing I discovered was that the executive director had not quit; she had been fired for theft. In addition, the bookkeeper was stealing also; she had forged some checks. When the bookkeeper got caught, she destroyed a whole year's worth of deposit slips and bank records…just about everything she could get her hands on. Then the government notified us that the bookkeeper had not made the payroll tax deposits for a whole year. We owed them $28,000 plus $10,000 in penalties and interest right up front. We went on to find out that bills had not been paid, including the lease on the copy machine and the phone lease."

It is not uncommon for both financial and membership records to be in a state of disarray when an association is in decline. It is virtually impossible to draft an emergency turnaround plan until these two houses are put back in order.

Staffing Issues

Get to know the staff as well as you can immediately, particularly in a small association. Mary Jane Kolar asks in advance that each employee provide her with a brief written report describing his or her responsibilities, background, the status of projects he or she is responsible for, and how he or she contributes to the overall mission of the association. Then she schedules an interview with each employee as soon as she arrives on the scene to complete an initial assessment.

Gene Bergoffen, CAE, president and CEO of the National Private Truck Council (NPTC), does this as well, and he assigns staff members to various task forces to deal with specific turnaround tasks. Bergoffen, who had been on the receiving end of turnarounds twice before he took the NPTC assignment, say he was particularly conscious of the people part of the turnaround.

"You have to be careful not to reorganize the staff too quickly," Bergoffen warns. "You have to test different things. You have to see your staff do different things in different environments. How they relate to others. How they write. How they speak. How they analyze. How they understand the depth of their programs. How open they are. How flexible they are. Who they relate to in the membership. You've got a lot of stuff to take note of before you make your key decisions."

Sooner or later you are going to have to cut staff in a turnaround situation, Bergoffen says, and it is critical that you cut the right people. "Everybody knows who the performers are when you do this," he adds. "You are either validating that you've made good sense within the bulk of the staff that remains, or that you've not recognized the true problems. So that's a very critical stage."

Program Analysis

The next step is to analyze the association's programs and services. Schedule an in-depth meeting with each staff person who is responsible for a program. Divide the meeting into two parts—one qualitative and one quantitative. The qualitative portion of the meeting deals with issues such as relevance of the program to the association's mission and strategic plan; evidence, if any, that the membership is pleased with the program; and how the membership might react if the program or service were discontinued as part of the stabilization plan.

The quantitative portion of the meeting would look hard at the numbers:

- Income and expense
- Numbers of members served
- Amount of staff time involved
- Changes that might boost the income and/or reduce the expenses

The objective is to determine those services that the association must continue to offer if it is to exist. Talk to your board members and other opinion leaders within the association. Where possible, meet with members, either individually or in small groups, and ask them to identify those services the organization must offer to retain the bulk of its members.

You may be surprised at the results. Over time, associations tend to add services without eliminating any of them. The typical member looks to the association to provide one or two services. The rest constitute pages in a catalog of merchandise they seldom buy.

It is like going to a resort that offers golf, tennis, a game room, a bowling alley, a swimming pool, an exercise room, free movies in the auditorium at night, and volleyball tournaments on the beach. Each service may be important and adds value to a segment of the customers, however small. Yet virtually all of its guests come primarily to play golf or tennis. The rest of the package is of lesser value, and to a majority of customers it is extraneous.

By the same token, the association may publish a magazine, a membership directory, and several how-to books. It may conduct two or three surveys of the industry. It may put on an annual convention, a fall conference, three or four special-interest seminars, and a school. It may have a government relations operation and a specialized library. Naturally, a sizable staff is required to plan and implement these services.

Few associations have a sophisticated cost-accounting system that tracks the amount of staff time and other general office resources, such as funds that must be spent on photocopying equipment and telephone, that are spent on each project. So while specific projects may appear to be profitable on the association's income statement, closer examination often reveals that many of them actually operate at a loss. After all, one of the reasons not-for-profits exist is to provide services that are not feasible in the for-profit sector.

As a result of your investigation, you may find that the only essential elements of your association are an annual convention, a monthly magazine, and the membership directory. The rest are like the exercise room, the bowling alley, and the volleyball tournament on the beach—nice to have, but if eliminated, will not cause significant numbers of members to resign.

By focusing on these must-have services, management can then reassess the entire headquarters operation. Instead of ten employees, perhaps the slimmed-down program can be carried out by two staff members. Or the organization might do away with the standalone headquarters altogether and move into a shared-resources operation, such as an association management firm or a shared-office facility.

The members will understand. After all, chances are that the entire industry is under siege, and everyone is cutting back. Members will applaud the cutbacks at their association as part of the pain-sharing process. Many, in fact, may retain their memberships as an expression of support for their association in its hour of need if they are convinced that managers are taking appropriate corrective steps.

In recent years, associations have been increasingly relying on nondues income to sustain the operation. In a downturn, two things typically happen to the association: membership declines, thereby lowering dues income; and sales of products and services fall off, reducing nondues income. The result is that the staff and administrative expenses are not matched by the income, and reserves are tapped to make up the difference.

Psychologically, both for the staff and for the volunteer leadership, there is an overwhelming temptation to expand the menu of services and to promote them ever more vigorously in a vain attempt to increase sales and memberships. This is a potentially fatal mistake that must be avoided. Until the association is operating within its means, it cannot expend the staff and volunteer time and other resources required to analyze the causes for the decline and to take the necessary steps to resurrect the association. If the experience of corporate turnarounds has taught us anything, it is that in a turnaround situation, downsizing and cutbacks are called for—not forays into new services.

Although cutting out programs will diminish the association's nondues revenue, to the extent that the products and services were offered for sale to the industry, this program reduction is unlikely to have a serious impact on dues revenue. This does not mean that membership and dues revenue will not continue the downward slope it was already on, because that is caused by other factors. But the fact that the headquarters operation was dramatically reduced will largely be transparent to the members, and inertia should buy the executive some time to turn the association around.

> **Turnaround Tip No. 6**
>
> "Get really, really, really good people and let them do their job. Turn 'em loose. That's one of the big keys."
>
> —**Dennis Jorgensen**
>
> Chief Operating Officer, American Marketing Association

As I look back on my experiences with FIMA, I now recognize that the failure to discontinue some programs and to focus on a few essential services at the outset of my tenure was extremely costly. It resulted in seriously diminishing the reserves that had been built up for more than a quarter of a century.

Drafting the Turnaround Plan

When an association's survival is at stake, certain long-term expenditures that would be prudent in normal times are now deemed to be extravagant. Travel to "show the flag" at related associations, for example, is perfectly reasonable when the association can afford it, but it is out of the question when the association is in a turnaround situation.

The association-owned automobile provided to the CEO is certainly a target for elimination, as is the cellular phone assigned to the CEO. The board of directors must take some hit as well. That association-paid dinner for board members and their spouses at the annual meeting now becomes a Dutch treat gathering in the hotel coffee shop. Magazine subscriptions, association dues, and attendance at workshops on building staff morale also show up on the hit list.

The place to start the turnaround budget is with dues income. Even here, it pays to be pessimistic. If membership has been declining, then assume that it will continue to decline until after stabilization has occurred.

Then staff salaries and headquarters operations—plus those services normally provided free to members, such as the monthly newsletter and the annual membership directory—must be covered by pessimistically anticipated dues income.

In a turnaround situation, the association CEO must do what is essential for survival. If it means cutting ten employees down to two, moving from a Class A office building to a windowless office in a renovated warehouse, reducing the number of incoming telephone lines down from eight to two, and eliminating free coffee for the staff, then that's what needs to be done.

Once you know the extent of your staff and administrative facilities, then you can take a look at the association's program of work. Suddenly those marginal projects, such as the free information center or that calendar of 10 two-day seminars, become impractical.

Keep in mind, however, that if you propose an overhead meltdown, it is important to operate the remaining services in a first-rate manner. If the annual convention, for example, is the only meeting conducted by the association during the year, it ought to be executed with class. When members attend the convention, they should come away with the impression that this organization has finally put its act together.

The plan you will present to the board will probably, but not necessarily, call for a scaled-down association that is operating within its means in a manner that is looked on with favor by its members and prospective members. If the job is done right, the bleeding should stop, and the rebirth should be ready to begin.

Achieving Volunteer Buy-In

However, the plan at this point is only a draft. Turnaround executives interviewed agreed that, for the plan to come together, there must be buy-in from the volunteer leadership, starting with the officers. If the current chief elected officer and the chief-elect are supportive, the chances of board approval are markedly improved. The executive may want to bring these key officers into the office for a day-long meeting to review each aspect of the plan, anticipating areas that might be controversial when presented before the full board. Ideally, the chief elected officer, as chair of the board, should lead the board discussion and should be an ardent supporter of the plan.

Once the plan has been amended so that both the chief and the chief-elect are its advocates, then the plan should be distributed in an advance mailing to the full board. The plan should be accompanied by a detailed memo from the executive director that addresses perceived controversial elements of the plan.

J. C. "Chris" Mahaffey, CAE, who serves as executive director of the Chicago Society of Association Executives, is adamant that the executive should lay his or her cards on the table in advance, so that there is no misunderstanding about where he or she stands on issues that come before the board.

"I don't see execs as a rule doing that," he admits, "but I think that's what they're being paid to do. You might alienate certain factions, but that's what's called being a leader."

If there is no strategic plan, or board-approved mission and vision, then the executive should create one in his or her draft, as a means of getting the board to focus on what kind of an organization it wants to be. Members of the board may want to wordsmith these elements when they discuss the plan at the meeting, and that should be encouraged.

The board's primary responsibility is to lead the organization down a desired path. Without board discussion and buy-in about these critical elements, the executive is in danger of moving an organization in a direction the volunteer leadership does not support. And that is a path to disaster for both the executive and the organization.

Operating on Two Fronts

Once the organization has stabilized the financial drain, there is a tendency to relax and declare the turnaround to be complete. But the scaled-down organization cannot be counted on to carry the day indefinitely. It is in a holding pattern; it must quickly evolve into a new organization, with a written mission statement, measurable objectives, and a strategic and tactical plan that will carry the organization forward.

This means that the organization must be operating on two fronts at once. It must operate its current program in a first-rate manner, and it must redesign the new organization, and rather quickly, at that. To help accomplish this, staff should be divided into two parts—one part keeps the current program of the association moving along, while the other part works to redesign the association.

If the staff is small, the redesign group might consist of the chief executive and a committee of volunteers, including the out-going and in-coming chief elected officers, as well as some other members of the board of directors. A larger organization might include more staff members on this transition team.

The staff member chosen to keep the train running should be a highly valued staff member who is given assurances that he or she will play a key role in the new organization. The last thing you want is for the executive who's running the show to be unsure about his or her status in the newly structured organization.

The executive chosen to be the operational manager must devise a budget that is broken down into monthly increments, to measure performance against expectations each month. With a scaled-down program, of course, the budget is greatly simplified. The operational executive's objective is simple, as well. It is to build reserves, if possible, but certainly to avoid further losses.

It is beyond the purview of this book to provide a primer on strategic planning. Not only are there entire volumes devoted to this topic, but there are a number of management consultants who specialize in helping associations to articulate their vision of the future and to develop plans for moving toward that vision.

For the purpose of keeping the association's program going while the long-term strategies are being developed, simplicity should be the byword. Typically, three to five simple strategies should be identified to accomplish each objective, with clearly enunciated tactics that are likely to employ the strategies successfully.

The tactics should be carefully worded in a way that they can be clearly monitored and measured. Results cannot be managed, but tactics can and must be.

For example, an objective might be to achieve 200 paid registrants for the annual conference. That is a result that is desired and anticipated. But it cannot be managed. It is the result of strategies successfully executed.

What can be managed is the tactic that states, "Develop the conference brochure and mail it to the full membership and 1,000 additional prospects by November 7." That's a tactic that can be measured, monitored, and achieved.

In short, objectives are desired results; strategies are methods selected to achieve those results; tactics are action plans for implementing the strategies:

1. Objectives are desires.

2. Strategies are methods.

3. Tactics are action steps.

In a typical association, the board is responsible for setting objectives. The chief paid executive is the member of the board who is authorized to devise strategies for achieving those objectives and for ensuring that the staff executes the tactics.

Objectives are measurable, as are the tactics. Strategies may or may not be. For example, an objective may be to increase total membership by 10 percent—from 1,000 members to 1,100 members—by January 1. One of the strategies may be to employ a member-get-a-member campaign. One of the tactics may be to mail details of the plan to all members by April 1.

The board should evaluate the objectives (i.e., the desired results). Did membership equal or exceed 1,100 on January 1? If so, the objective was met.

If membership falls short, then the board should ask if the tactics were carried out. If the details of the member-get-a-member campaign were not mailed to all members by April 1, then the chief executive has some explaining to do.

But if all the tactical goals pertaining to the membership objective were successfully executed, then the board and the chief executive need to examine the strategies in an atmosphere of cooperation. What went right? What went wrong? What changes need to be made? Perhaps they will conclude that the right strategies were employed, but that the objective was unrealistic.

In a turnaround situation, you should be careful to ensure that objectives can be measured throughout the year. The membership objective discussed earlier, for example, might be broken down to four quarterly objectives (e.g., 1,025 members by April 1; 1,050 by July 1; 1,075 by October 1; and 1,100 by January 1).

> **Turnaround Tip No. 7**
>
> "If you have to do something bad, do it all at once. If you are doing something good, do a little good every year so that the Board will remember the good that you have done."
>
> —**Robert E. Becker, J.D., CAE**
>
> President, Bostrom Corporation

In the meantime, the turnaround team is turning its attention to reinventing the organization. In the process, it will explore a myriad options for aligning the association with the changing needs of its newly defined membership.

The first 60 days of the turnaround are critical. Appendix A presents a sample plan for the first eight weeks. The plan assumes that the chief executive officer is new to the organization and has been granted 60 days to develop and to present to the board a turnaround plan.

4 | Options for Organizational Change

By now, you have talked to staff, board members, and nonboard industry leaders, as well as your network of association executives and volunteer leaders who may have faced similar situations. You have examined the business theory of your association and have concluded that there is a need for your organization to exist. The mission is not only a valid one, but it is clearly understood by volunteer leaders and paid staff alike. Now it is time to choose a course of action.

Dozens of association executives who have been through turnaround situations were interviewed for this book. They proposed a wide array of options; however, these options tend to fall into four categories:

- Organizational options
- Program options
- Financial options
- Communications options

This chapter will focus on organizational options. (The other options are discussed in subsequent chapters.) Organizational options involve changes that might be made to the structure of the organization, including governance, membership, staff, and headquarters operation.

Governance

When a turnaround is indicated, the organization must be prepared to make prudent changes quickly. Yet, organizations formed at a time when change was slow will have built-in impediments to change.

As Philip Lesser, CAE, of the Bostrom Corporation says: "If you wanted to design an organization that was inefficient, and an organization that could not respond quickly to the environment, you'd come up with the way we run associations. You'd have a volunteer board that is clueless. You'd have an executive director who has little power. You couldn't design from scratch anything that would be more inefficient or more conservative…powerless bureaucrats following uninformed volunteers."

For this reason, Mary Jane Kolar, CAE, advises executives to read thoroughly the association's bylaws, as well as its policies and procedures documents, to determine what land mines may be waiting to impede the turnaround process.

"You can learn an awful lot," she contends, "from a review of [an association's] fundamental documents. Many times [these associations] have been forced to get sick because the seeds of destruction are planted in the bylaws." She suggests that turnaround executives consider the following questions:

- How is the president (or chair) elected? Is it strictly a popularity contest at the annual meeting, or is there a provision for a nominating committee to meet in advance to give serious consideration to candidates or to recruit well-qualified people to assume leadership positions?

> **Turnaround Tip No. 8**
>
> "Don't wait until it's apparent that you're in a turnaround situation. Many organizations are in the position that if one or two things should occur, it would put them in dire straits. You must be careful of assuming that an organization with a long history is well positioned, for in many cases they're not, and it would take only one little thing to upset the apple cart and the organization could find itself in great trauma."
>
> **—Jeffry W. Raynes, CAE**
>
> Executive Director and Chief Operating Officer, American Production and Inventory Control Society, Inc.

- How are the various classes of membership defined? Do the classifications offer flexibility to shift the association's direction, if need be? Do they reflect changes going on in the industry or profession served?
- What are the roles of the officers and board members? How are the chief staff officer's responsibilities defined?
- Is an executive committee clearly designated and authorized to make decisions between board meetings? Is there a provision for the executive committee's decisions to be ratified by the full board?
- What about standing committees? Are committees included in the bylaws that ought to be left to the discretion of the board or executive committee to establish as conditions warrant? Generally speaking, the only committees that should be listed in the bylaws are the executive committee, finance committee, and the nominating committee. Other committees, if any, should exist at the pleasure of the board.
- What items require a majority, or even a super majority, vote of the board, executive committee, or membership to change? Will this impede the ability to implement needed changes quickly?

A thorough reading of the bylaws, Kolar suggests, can reveal several areas where changes need to be made. And those changes should be recommended to the board in the executive's initial plan of action for the turnaround.

Committees

Mention the word "committee" to an association executive, and a lengthy discussion is likely to follow. Committees, properly organized and managed, can be the lifeblood of the organization. On the other hand, they can impede progress and facilitate the destruction of an organization.

Often, an executive in a turnaround will face the need to dissolve committees, particularly standing committees. When Donald E. Manger took over as president/CEO of the Treasury Management Association, he found the organization was saddled with committees that met without any clear purpose.

"Whenever you have a group of people that don't have a clear mission," he notes, "they thrash about trying to find something to do to accomplish, for they want to feel like they're being useful, too. And that isn't helpful for the organization. I was very fortunate that I had a leadership that was willing to run interference and would support me when I asked them to disband a committee."

With tongue planted firmly in cheek, Kolar contends the motto of some association committees is "Ever Onward, Never Finished." She feels that committees tend to be ineffective because their stated purpose as a committee tends to be process-oriented, rather than results-oriented. "That's absolutely deadly in this day and age," she says. "You absolutely cannot survive and thrive based on that method of operation."

Effective committees have clearly defined objectives, with firmly established time lines. They can be useful for specific tasks during a turnaround, but unwanted and unneeded committees stand in the way and need to be abolished, which is exactly what Frederick D. Hunt, Jr., did when he assumed the presidency of the Society of Professional Benefit Administrators (SPBA). SPBA had run into financial troubles and was given three months to live by the previous executive director. Hunt cites three reasons for abolishing standing committees:

1. They are costly to meet and support, yet they tend to get mired in their own interests and bureaucracy.

2. They often are a hindrance, or are viewed as such, to new talent and new ideas.
3. They pose a legal liability when they assume the power to speak for the association.

He convinced the board that it should act as a committee of the whole to deal with any substantive issue that formerly would have been handled by a standing committee. To gain the flexibility needed in a turnaround, and to tap the energies and enthusiasm of the members, Hunt forms task forces that last anywhere "from 20 minutes to two years."

Hunt explains how it works:

"When a person calls me and says 'SPBA oughta…,' I make the decision on the spot whether it makes any sense. If so, I (or the chairman) may appoint the person as head of a task force to investigate and report back to me for the board, thus avoiding any final committee statements or opinions.

"The advantage is that any member is as close as his [or her] phone to taking a leadership role in the association on any issue he/she feels deserves attention. The advantages to SPBA are important. We get free experts doing the research. The person calling presumably has some expertise to have spotted the issue. He/she also probably has some motivation to have made the effort to call.

"If a second person calls on the same issue, we tell them to hook up with the first person. If it is an issue that relates to board past/present/future deliberations, I insert a board member in the task force loop.

"A bonus advantage is that a member who has some gung-ho idea discovers, himself, why it would not work. Thus he is satisfied, and not feeling that the association didn't give his idea a fair shake. In any case, about 30 percent of SPBA's member firms can congratulate themselves on having played an active leadership role each year on any issue important to them."

Membership

There are several options to consider regarding the structure of your membership base.

Take in vendor members. Virtually every group of members with a common interest has spawned a group of businesses that sell products and services to those members. Consequently, these vendors are interested in the welfare of the association. Too often, associations look on these businesses with disdain, but in a turnaround situation, they can represent salvation for the association.

Rather than treating vendor members as a source of contributions, forward-thinking associations tap into the expertise of these members. Typically, they are a source of valuable information about the trials and tribulations of your members. Consider them as potential board members and officers. As a group, they tend to function well on committees and task forces, bringing a valuable perspective to the deliberations.

Expand your member base. There is a lot to be said for a narrow focus, but it is possible for that focus to be too narrow, particularly in a changing industry. As the structure of the organizations served by your membership changes, look for new categories of members who are not presently served well by other associations.

If the Savings Institutions Marketing Society of America—an organization of savings-and-loan and mutual savings bank marketers—had not opened its membership to credit unions in the mid-1980s, changing its name in the process to the Financial Institutions Marketing Association, it is unlikely that the association could have survived the widespread failures of savings and loans in 1989 and 1990 that virtually wiped out the thrift industry. By 1995, credit union marketers represented more than one-third of the membership, while the number of savings and loans continued to shrink through mergers and acquisitions.

> **Turnaround Tip No. 9**
>
> "To build your credibility with the Board, keep them aware of the financial situation on a monthly basis. Show them what's working and what's not."
>
> **—Richard Bagin**
>
> Executive Director, National School Public Relations Association

Focus on member retention without neglecting new-member recruitment. When an association is experiencing difficulties, the membership development focus should shift toward greater emphasis on member retention. Potential new members want to identify with a winner, and it may be difficult to project that image when you are under siege. Present members are more likely to feel a sense of ownership in the association and are more likely to continue their support of the organization in its hour of need. To foster this sense of ownership and encourage support, the association needs to initiate open and honest communication on a frequent and regular basis. Involve as many members as possible on committees and task forces that are working at solving the association's problems. The vendor community can be particularly helpful at this stage.

Restructure in a way that enhances the ability of the organization to make changes. In the book, *Restructuring and Turnaround: Experiences in Corporate Renewal* (1987), an unidentified consultant was quoted as saying: "Most people think that the best way to run a large organization is to reduce the risk of error by establishing lots of rules, policies, and administrative procedures. The trouble is that these create a change-proof environment. Over time, change is even regarded with suspicion. But what most companies need to do is change—sometimes dramatically—to keep up, or even to survive."

Staff

Certainly one of the most difficult aspects of turnaround management is dealing fairly and compassionately with the association's staff. Usually, some positions must be eliminated if the association is to survive. It would be nice if this could be accomplished by attrition, but that seldom happens.

During the decline that led to the turnaround crisis, your staff had to work harder than ever at jobs that became increasingly tough and stressful. If anything, their salaries deserve to be doubled. In reality, one or more of them must be dismissed.

Ironically, the two biggest mistakes turnaround executives confessed to making in staff relations were acting too fast or acting too slowly. The corporate turnaround literature advises that staff downsizing be carried out quickly so that the surviving staff can go about the difficult tasks involved in turning the organization around. People who are worried about the continued existence of their jobs will spend a considerable amount of time networking with their friends and associates on the outside in hopes of landing a new job quickly if their present job should disappear. A winning team must enjoy high staff morale or it is defeated before the game begins.

Nevertheless, Jeffry W. Raynes, CAE, executive director and chief operating officer of the American Production and Inventory Control Society, gives this warning: "The challenge sometimes with crisis management is to avoid the urge to rebuild without rethinking. Don't just come in and reorganize without giving much thought to the implications of that reorganization."

Raynes says it is like managing a Little League™ baseball team. "You have all the accountability, but the players have all the responsibility. If they don't meet their goals, you won't meet yours."

David E. Poisson, CAE, turned the office into an outplacement agency after he took over as executive director of the Computer Dealers and Lessors Association. But he did not take this action until after the board had engaged in a strategic planning session and had determined that downsizing was necessary.

"I am prepared to work with you to find suitable alternate employment," he promised his staff after the board had made its decision. Poisson counseled his employees individually and used his own extensive contacts within the Washington association community to help them network to new jobs, and the results were favorable. "Everyone ended up in good jobs with comparable or better salaries," he declares.

Firing one person is distasteful enough to a manager, but when you have to release several staff at the same time, there is no easy way to do it. David M. Patt, CAE, tells of his experience in downsizing the Chicago Area Runners Association when he took over as its executive director in 1990: "We were operating on three floors.... My office was on the top floor with no duct work. Although connected to the lower floors by a stairway, the top floor had no heating or air-conditioning. Consequently, I would work at home in the morning, but, of course, I had to come to the office to dismiss someone, and I would ask them to come up to my office. So the reputation spread among the staff that when you were called to my office, you were going to be fired."

Jeffry Raynes reminds executives that their own jobs are not immune, either. "There are many difficult decisions to make in a turnaround," he says, "and if you base your decisions on your tenure with the organization, then you have lost before you start. You've got to be willing to say, 'I can find another job someplace,' for there are times when it gets incredibly difficult.

"You'll take a lot of heat from certain segments of the membership, for not everyone will understand the change. Half

> **Turnaround Tip No. 10**
>
> "The first two or three weeks I stayed in the office, but you need to get out and talk to members and nonmembers, as well as people who relate to and work with the association. You have to determine what the values are. You've got to find the truth, and you can't find the truth in any one dimension without finding the truth in other dimensions as well."
>
> **—Gene Bergoffen, CAE**
>
> President and CEO, National Private Truck Council

will like it and half will not, and I can guarantee you that the half that doesn't will be louder than the half that does."

When faced with downsizing, it is important for the executive to put his or her position in the proper perspective. Most executives feel they are part of the staff and that they report to the board of directors. In a turnaround, it is better for the executive to think of himself or herself not as a member of the staff, but rather as a member of the board who has been delegated the responsibility of managing the staff.

Except in rare situations, it is not the mission of the organization to provide interesting and lucrative jobs for staff. Rather, the organization belongs to its members, whose needs and desires are paramount. While one should deal with staff fairly and compassionately, your primary allegiance must be to the members, through their representatives on the board, even if your own job must be sacrificed in the process.

Shared Resources

If your association is functioning on a standalone basis, renting office space and employing a full complement of staff, a move into a shared-resources operation can reduce operating expenses significantly, with minimal disruption to the association's program.

Most major cities have companies that provide shared-office arrangements. They feature private offices, fully or partially furnished, that are rented out to their clients. These clients often share office amenities, such as a conference room, mailing equipment, receptionist, photocopying machine, employee lounge, and even computer equipment.

Such an arrangement is particularly attractive in a turnaround situation, because it can constitute an effective short-term bridge between the old structure and the new. Suppose, for example, it is necessary to cut staff from fifteen to three, but that the reinvented association might eventually require eight or ten staff members. The shared office, rented on a month-by-month basis, could accommodate the association during the transition from the old fifteen-person staff to the new ten-person organization. After the new structure is firmly established, the association could then reconsider a standalone operation.

A variation of the shared-office concept is one in which the association secures office space from another association, perhaps in a related field. The advantage of this arrangement is that the organization can also "rent" some of the staff expertise of the umbrella organization in areas such as accounting, human resources, product sales, and membership file maintenance.

Particularly useful to troubled associations is the full-service association management firm, whose staff provide full-service management for multiple associations. In this arrangement, the management firm provides all functions of the association's management and operations, including a complete staff, from the executive director on down, in a shared-resources capacity. A single executive director might manage the affairs of as many as five separate organizations, with staff functions "purchased" on an hourly basis from the specialists employed by the firm.

When the Financial Institutions Marketing Association became a full-service client of Smith, Bucklin, and Associates, Inc., the Chicago-based management firm interviewed all six employees of the association and hired four of them—two as fulltime managers of the account and the other two in other departments of the firm, thereby reducing severance costs and providing jobs for downsized employees. The association was then in a position to select from more than 600 employees of the company to carry out its program of work.

Often, a move to a management firm is transparent to the membership. In fact, it often gives the impression that the association's staff has been somewhat enlarged, because several individuals are listed as staff in the membership directory, even though many of them work only a few hours a month on that association's affairs. Putting the administrative hassles into the hands of a management firm also frees up the association's board to concentrate on substantive issues, particularly important during a turnaround, instead of spending valuable time discussing matters such as staff salaries, hiring/firing, rent, computer purchases, and the color of the new office carpet.

Chris Mahaffey, CAE, of the Chicago Society of Association Executives observes that one of the biggest changes in the makeup of the association community in Chicago in recent years has been the growth of association management firms. They tend to thrive in both a down and an up economy. When general economic conditions are poor, many standalone associations find refuge in the association management firm. Then, when economic conditions improve, the billings of the company grow with the increased activity.

In addition to providing a large measure of flexibility for a small association, many management firms also offer their expertise in targeted areas on a contract basis. This provides another option for the standalone association in that it can maintain a small staff to carry out its day-to-day activities and contract with a management firm to work on specific projects, such as the annual meeting. Or it can outsource to the firm functions such as accounting, membership surveys, telemarketing, and newsletter production.

A twist on the association management firm concept is one in which the association farms out its expertise to other associations. Or where the association provides management service for smaller segments of its membership that wish to

> **Turnaround Tip No. 11**
>
> "I think the most important thing we learned was the value of planning. It was the breaking up of a family. We tried to take a humane approach and was fully supported by the Board. While it was very trying, we can all look back and appreciate the way we handled it."
>
> —David E. Poisson, CAE
>
> Account Executive, Smith, Bucklin & Associates, Inc.

have organizations of their own. These special interest groups can help absorb office overhead expenses while retaining member loyalty to the parent group.

Smaller Office Space

Another option to reduce office expenses is to move the office into smaller quarters. Although this may lower the rent payments, an office move can be disrupting and time-consuming, especially if the organization needs to dispose of furniture. If you try to sell office furniture on a direct basis, that $1,000 executive desk will probably sell for only $100 or so. Most metropolitan areas have dealers in used office furniture who will purchase your furnishings and pick them up. But depending on the volume and quality of your furnishings, you are likely to recover little, if any, additional working cash.

And that's only the tip of the iceberg. Telephones and computers must be taken down and reinstalled. All of your brochures will need to be reprinted with the new address, and new letterhead and business cards will need to be printed. Cleaning out the files, making a determination of what to discard and what to keep, is a time-consuming and unpleasant task to be performed at a time when staff's energies and enthusiasm need to be directed toward more important turnaround tasks.

In some cases, your office lease may preclude you from moving. It is important to consult the association's attorney and talk to the building management. Building management may be willing to reduce the space you occupy, provide storage space for files and furnishings, and even rewrite the lease on more favorable terms to protect and preserve its long-term relationship with your association.

Merger or Affiliation

Just because you have determined there is a reason for your association to exist does not necessarily mean it is best that you continue as an independent organization, especially if your market is in a state of flux. There may well be another organization whose strengths would mesh well with yours. Perhaps you put on great conferences, but your government relations capability is weak; while a sister organization might enjoy a strong lobbying force but tends to sport a weak educational program. Theoretically, if you merged the two, you'd be strong in both areas.

In actual practice, however, egos tend to rule when it comes to merging two not-for-profit organizations. Board members with ambitions of becoming officers may fear that their leadership pipeline will be disrupted. Cultures collide when a staff-driven association attempts to merge with a member-driven group. Staffs clash over headquarters responsibilities. Unless one executive director is ready to retire, there is jockeying for the chief staff officer's position. Frustrated boards occasionally declare both executive directors off-limits and launch a search for an "objective" third party to manage the staff.

How do you merge two libraries, when one is using cutting-edge online research technology while the other is sorting magazine clippings in manila folders arranged alphabetically by subject? What do you do about the annual meeting, when Group A traditionally meets in the winter at a golfing resort in Arizona, while Group B hunkers down in a big city convention hotel? And how can you agree on the name of the merged organization, when both groups have generated thousands of members over the years whose personal identity is tied to an acronym that defies pronunciation?

Creative thinkers *have* found it possible to merge two organizations and still retain identity, staffs, and separate cultures. One such group is the Bank Marketing Association (BMA), which made the shift from a standalone association to an affiliate of the industry's giant American Bankers Association (ABA).

Founded in 1915 as the Financial Advertisers Association, BMA's members are marketing executives of financial institutions, primarily commercial banks. In 1983, its reading of the external environment suggested that banks, savings and loan associations, and credit unions were evolving into a single financial services industry. Its staff and volunteer leaders projected that the number of financial institutions was likely to diminish, with corresponding negative effects on membership—an assumption that ultimately proved to be true.

Even though it was financially strong, with liquid reserves of about $2 million, and its membership was stable, the leadership of the association perceived the potential for trouble and took steps to prepare itself for such a scenario.

At the same time, ABA, the largest trade association in the banking field, was observing similar trends, but was also recognizing that deregulation of the industry would enhance the need for marketing expertise among its member institutions, and ABA's marketing education program was relatively weak. In the words of ABA's executive director, Willis W. Alexander, "we either had to build it (a marketing program) or buy it." The elected leadership of the two associations met to discuss an arrangement that would benefit both groups.

The result was an affiliation, whereby ABA established a not-for-profit organization under the laws of Delaware to be known as the Bank Marketing Association. Its bylaws, for the most part a duplicate of those of the existing BMA (incorporated in Illinois), contained two significant changes:

- The Executive Committee of ABA would be the organization's only voting member.

- All of BMA's assets would be the property of ABA, and the treasurer of ABA would automatically become a member of the board and the executive committee of BMA, thereby establishing a governance link between the two groups.

Then BMA (Illinois) was merged into the newly formed BMA (Delaware), effectively combining the two organizations

> **Turnaround Tip No. 12**
>
> "I did make one smart move. I thought I wanted my own bookkeeper, but then I outsourced our bookkeeping, and that was a good move. I found a small, two-person accounting firm. That made it affordable. But I started out by trying to hire a fulltime bookkeeper. I never should have done that."
>
> —**Michael T. Dunham**
>
> Executive Vice President, Georgia Branch, Associated General Contractors of America, Inc.

into the not-for-profit equivalent of a wholly owned subsidiary. BMA continued to operate with its existing staff, headed by Executive Vice President Raymond M. Cheseldine, from its Chicago headquarters. Over the next few years, in a continuing effort to reduce operational redundancies, various functions were absorbed by the Washington-based ABA, enabling BMA to reduce its sixty-five-person staff to about forty-five without adversely affecting its service to members in any noticeable way.

Eventually, the association's headquarters was moved to ABA offices in Washington, thereby maximizing the operating economies of the affiliation and enabling the association to provide its full range of services with a reduced staff of about twenty-five.

Such arrangements are a rarity. More often, mergers constitute a last-resort attempt to save what is left of a failing association. In that case, the strong partner takes over the turnaround candidate and absorbs its staff and members into the surviving organization.

Occasionally, two weak associations in the same industry will combine in an effort to shore up each other in an industry that is shrinking. But often that produces a new association that is itself a turnaround candidate.

Nevertheless, whether one calls it a merger, an affiliation, or an alliance, the concept of joining two or more organizations together for mutual support, even if only partially, is an option available to resolve a turnaround situation.

5 | Program Options

Prospective members of an association often will ask its leadership: "What do I get as a member?" The answer typically involves a program of products and services that addresses prospective members' needs and concerns. These benefits may range from "ways to make my business more successful" to "helps make my community a better place in which to live."

Over time, these programs build up, with each program consuming a share, however large or small, of available staff resources. In fact, additional staff often is needed to continue offering services at a high-quality level. Soon, some of these programs reach the peak of their product cycle and begin to decline. Yet, the association keeps offering the service because it has been around so long it has become a fixture. Besides, if some members are still using the service, why discontinue it? And doesn't the income statement indicate that the service generates a profit?

When a financial crisis hits, the association shifts into turnaround mode. Net income from fee-based services, plus dues income, fails to equal the expense of salaries and overhead, and the association's reserve fund quickly begins to shrink.

This is when, as described in Chapter 3, downsizing occurs and the list of association services is pared down to its core. Simple in theory as this may be, it does not apply to all circumstances. There are documented instances when the addition of services helps provide income to reverse the downtrend.

Take the Society of Professional Journalists (SPJ), for example. When Executive Director Gregory A. Christopher moved into the chief staff officer's position in 1993, the organization, comprised mainly of newspaper reporters and editors, plus a large number of journalism professors, had already declined from a peak of 20,000-plus members in the early 1980s to about 12,500. This decline can be largely attributed to the closing of daily newspapers and the merging of other news media.

In reaction, the society reduced its staff and its services to the point where about all it offered its members were a monthly magazine, *The Quill*, and an annual convention that was also in decline. "There was a phrase tossed around the organization," Christopher says, "that the only thing you got for your dues was a Quill and a bill."

In his situation, retrenching was no longer an option. They'd been there and done that, and it hadn't worked. "My view on SPJ," said Christopher, "was that we had no message out there; we had no visibility, no outreach plan. We were pretty much running from year to year doing the same old things. We needed to be aggressive, and we needed to get our name out there."

To get back into the game, Christopher orchestrated a series

> **Turnaround Tip No. 13**
>
> "I really do believe that the wave of the future for association survival is nondues sources of income, whatever that might be. It might be a magazine that generates a tremendous amount of money. It might be a trade show. It may be a different type of service. They could fund your services and lessen your dues. And that's the name of the game. If you want members, you've got to have competitive dues, and if you want competitive dues, you've got to find ways to fund the association outside the dues."
>
> **—John W. Boyd**
>
> Executive Vice President, Carolinas Electrical Contractors Association

of professional development workshops. To ease the financial burden and lessen the risk, he recruited corporate sponsors, such as daily newspaper publishers, to lend their good name and help defray some of the costs.

"These journalism organizations, we found, were not so much interested in giving money to SPJ just for general operating funds, but if you put the pitch in the tone that they're helping to improve journalism, and you gave them something concrete to look at, such as the workshop, it was much more attractive to them," Christopher says.

The society conducts ten to fifteen professional development workshops per year, attracting 250 to 500 registrants each. The workshops bring in revenue in three ways: workshop registration fees, paid dues from new members, and sales of merchandise and books. As a result, the society brought its fund balance from a low of $20,000 in 1992 to $235,000 in 1996.

Despite SPJ's success, expanding your program of work in a turnaround situation is considered risky business. New ventures often lose money before they make money. And, if the membership is declining, the market for publications and educational conferences is shrinking as well. A workshop budgeted to make $10,000 can easily lose $20,000 because most of the expenses are in planning and promotion.

Aside from firing staff, an association executive's next most unpleasant task is canceling a conference for lack of sufficient attendance. The members who already have registered have not only altered their personal and business schedules to attend the meeting, but they may have purchased nonrefundable airplane tickets for travel to the conference. Paid speakers often impose a cancellation penalty. Even larger penalties emanate from the hotel that set aside all those guest rooms that now will go empty.

By the same token, publications, such as books and magazines, absorb considerable upfront costs before they begin to pay off. So, miscalculations in those areas can hasten the demise of the troubled association.

Consultant Rodney S. Brutlag, CAE, who as an association executive successfully chaired the Educational Committee of the Chicago Society of Association Executives during its turnaround, is a strong advocate of conducting a needs assessment of members before investing in new products and services. Asking your members what they think of the association is helpful, but misses an important opportunity, in Brutlag's view. Instead, he suggests that you probe to find out what challenges or issues members are facing in their lives that the association might be able to address.

Brutlag likes to conduct focused interviews with small groups of members to help catalog a list of issues and possible association solutions for those issues. From these interviews, he crafts a questionnaire that can be mailed to the entire membership (or a random sample of a large membership) that can help identify those issues that are most important to members.

Many turnaround executives feel that the association's board of directors cannot realistically identify the most important issues facing the industry or profession, because board members seldom are representative of the rank-and-file of the membership.

With that caveat, here are some areas turnaround executives found to be helpful in crafting a turnaround program of work:

Conferences and Workshops. There's a reason why we refer to our organizations as "associations": A principal reason people join is to "associate" with others who share in similar activities or interests. In the Introduction, National School Public Relations Association's success in asking its past presidents to put on a workshop was used as an example. It not only represented the finest minds in school public relations, but the participants did it for free to help out the association in its hour of need.

Nancy C. Carleton, CAE, breathed life into the monthly

meetings of the Upstate New York Chapter of the International Association of Financial Planning by introducing what she calls "structured networking" to the chapter's meetings. About two-thirds of the tables are designated with different topics for discussion, moderated by a table host.

Members can either sit at one of these tables to discuss the designated topic, or they can sit at one of the nondesignated tables. "Back in the old days," Carleton recalls, "about five minutes after the meeting was over, people were gone. Now they are hanging around for a half hour or more, continuing their discussion." She credits the networking with helping turn the chapter around by increasing the attraction of chapter meetings to its members.

Chris Mahaffey was skeptical when the elected leadership of the Chicago Society of Association Executives proposed a luncheon and trade show in the middle of the hectic Christmas season and in competition with similar industry events. Dubbed "Holiday Showcase," the one-day event now brings in more than one-fourth of the society's annual revenues, more even than from member dues.

Publications. A magazine can bring in large revenues and provide unparalleled visibility for an organization, provided it can fill a void in the marketplace. The turnaround of the National Precast Concrete Association was enhanced by the introduction of *MC Magazine*. The magazine focuses narrowly on the precast concrete industry, a niche that was only superficially covered by existing magazines in the broader concrete industry. Not only has the magazine itself been profitable, reports President Ty E. Gable, CAE, but its distribution to nonmembers has raised the visibility of the association. It has helped to build new-member growth by 10 percent the year after the magazine's debut and increase the member retention rate from 82 percent to 93 percent.

Litigation. Sue the government and win. That was the turnaround solution for the Wisconsin Manufactured Housing

Association. Executive Director Ross P. Kinzler took over an association in 1989 that was stagnant and floundering. Members were so disinterested in the association that "during the first week I was there, no one called the office. The silence was scary," he says.

Because he knew little about the industry, having served formerly as associate director of a school boards association, Kinzler started making random calls to members to determine what their problems were. He found out that manufactured housing was getting short shrift from zoning boards, which often blocked attempts to build manufactured housing in their jurisdictions.

Kinzler got the idea of suing a municipality for discriminating against his members' product. "We bought a piece of property," he says, "and engaged a law firm to sit down with us and figure out a way to use this piece of property to bring a zoning discrimination suit against the city. We took pictures of all the neighboring homes and had plans drawn that looked just like those houses, but they were going to be built to our building code, not to the state's building code.

"We filed for the building permit, got denied, filed suit in court, and the court overturned the city's zoning decision. The rest is…history."

Winning the court case broke the floodgates and added about a thousand unit sales to the association's members' base per year. Because dues are related to sales, the additional business instantly escalated dues income.

"We had recaptured the amount of money that went into our lawsuit three times over by the end of the first year," Kinzler says. In addition, membership boomed, and attendance at association meetings increased. The association's budget before the lawsuit was about $180,000. After the lawsuit, it grew to more than $500,000. And now the office phone is ringing merrily once again.

6 Financial Options

A turnaround association is, by definition, in poor financial straits. Although it may enjoy a comfortable fund balance, those reserves can disappear quickly. Don't be like the man who jumps off a twenty-story building. As he passes a fifth floor window, someone asks how it's going, and he replies: "So far, so good."

There are four basic strategies to reverse a deteriorating financial situation:

1. Immediately implement cost reductions to stop the bleeding.
2. Use cash management techniques to speed up collections and slow down disbursements.
3. Revamp the infrastructure.
4. Increase revenues.

Before you begin, you should generate a cash-flow budget that details your expected revenues and disbursements on a month-by-month basis. For now, ignore accounting niceties, such as accounts receivable and accounts payable.

There's no question that monthly budgets are a pain. It is difficult to forecast exactly when a check will come in or when a bill needs to be paid. Nevertheless,

> **Turnaround Tip No. 14**
>
> "I recommend that anyone stepping into a turnaround situation should do what they can to improve staff morale. A happier, more satisfied work force can positively change matters."
>
> —**Walter W. Bacak, Jr.**
>
> Executive Director, American Translators Association

you should do it anyway, because it will give you a regular reading of your progress. It also will tell you whether you are prone to excessive optimism or excessive pessimism—both of which should be avoided.

Communicate this budget to your staff and to your volunteer leaders. Staff are undoubtedly nervous about the outlook for downsizing, and a cash-flow budget can be used as a motivational device that reinforces the need for increasing revenues and decreasing expenditures. If staff beat the forecast, they will feel comforted. If they consistently fall short, they will be better prepared psychologically for additional cutbacks.

Stop the Bleeding

The following short-term actions can show results almost immediately. Rarely will they be enough to reverse the fortunes of the association, but they will slow down the financial deterioration of the association:

1. **Reduce travel.** No one, even the executive director, should go anywhere out of town unless it is absolutely necessary, especially on site inspection trips. The American Marketing Association, for example, switched many of its committee meetings to telephone conferences.

2. **Reduce dues and subscriptions.** Association executives are incurable joiners. But when the patient is bleeding, you may have to say no when a dues notice arrives in the mail. By the same token, paid subscriptions to newspapers and magazines ought to be carefully reviewed. Is it necessary that you receive a copy of the

New York Times or the *Wall Street Journal* every morning? The answer may be yes, but it's a question that should be asked.

3. **Avoid overnight couriers.** Can the advance mailing to the board go by regular mail next time, rather than by Zippy Express?

4. **Review maintenance contracts.** Instead of paying for repairs in advance through maintenance contracts, wait until the copier or postage meter is broken and repaired before you pay to have it fixed.

5. **Review use of offsite storage.** You can probably dispose of much of your stored material and bring the rest in-house.

6. **Eliminate company-owned autos and cellular phones.** From now on, take a cab and use a pay phone.

7. **Review what you've outsourced.** Mailing services? Brochure copywriting? Newsletter production? Public relations activities? Can you bring any of it in-house?

8. **Evaluate office supply purchases.** Shop around; you may find some savings at office supply superstores or at a warehouse club.

9. **Negotiate with your suppliers.** You may be surprised at how many vendors are willing to shave 2 or 3 cents off an item you purchase in volume just because you asked and because they want you to succeed at the turnaround so you'll continue to be their customer. Elissa Passiment, executive director of the American Society for Clinical Laboratory Science, told her landlord that the society could not pay the rent on the 5,700 square feet they occupied, even though they were only in the third year of a ten-year lease. The landlord found them smaller space—2,100 square feet on a different floor of the same

building—and rented it to them for the cost of only 1,800 square feet.

10. **Say no to committee requests for spending.** Donald E. Manger, president/CEO of the Treasury Management Association, said that turning down committee requests for spending put the brakes on a lot of projects that weren't going to go anywhere. Frederick D. Hunt, Jr., president of the Society of Professional Benefit Administrators, created a mythical "Frugal Fred" who put a stop to many unnecessary spending requests of the volunteers.

11. **Review publications costs.** Can you cut down on the number of pages in your membership directory by reducing the type size? Would that four-color newsletter work as a one-color job? Can you combine two publications into one?

Cash Management Techniques

The whole idea behind cash management is to hasten the flow of cash into your association's bank account and to delay the flow out. The following are some techniques associations have used successfully.

Use a lock box. Most banks, for a small fee, offer a lock box service that cuts the time required to deposit a check into your account by a day or two. On invoices, advise members and others who pay their dues or purchase products and services to send their payments to a post office box (commonly referred to as a lock box). A bank employee opens the box each day and deposits the checks directly into the association's bank account. The bank then sends a copy of the check, along with any supporting documentation, to the association for processing. Many new executive directors have discovered drawers full of undeposited checks due to negligence on the part of staff. A loc box prevents this situation, and your money goes to work for you right away.

Send dues invoices early. Have you ever noticed that shortly after you subscribe to a magazine, you get a renewal notice that encourages you to renew your subscription now at today's rates? Circulation managers refer to this technique as "renewal at birth." You can use a similar technique with new members.

When you send a welcome letter to new members, you can give them the opportunity to extend their membership for another year or two, thereby avoiding any dues increase that might come up during the term. Renewal notices to existing members can go out as early as four months before the end of the fiscal year. Because most members pay their dues on the first notice, you can delay sending the second notice until two months before expiration. By giving that extra month, you reduce the number of checks that come in after the second notices have been prepared. On your association's balance sheet, these advance payments are listed on the liability side as deferred income, with no impact on the income statement for the present year. Nevertheless, these payments put cash in your association's bank account and can be used to pay bills.

Sell bonds. The Chicago Area Runners Association (CARA) created a two-year bond in $1,000 denominations, paying 8 percent interest, which it sold to its members. The association consulted a securities lawyer to ensure the plan would not run afoul of securities laws. CARA raised $25,000, which was ultimately paid off after the turnaround.

Aggressively collect receivables. Make a determined effort to collect money owed to the association. Place telephone calls to those who are more than 60 days in arrears. If necessary,

---

Turnaround Tip No. 15

"Identify and select and groom your Board members. Have the wherewithal to identify those members who ought to serve on the Board. You may not be able to control it, but you can certainly influence it."

—**Glenda Soyars**

President, Florida Employers Exchange, Inc.

suspend services of members who are seriously delinquent in paying the association monies owed to it.

Sell something. This technique is used frequently in the corporate sector, as corporations discover that the whole is worth less than the sum of its parts. If you have a magazine that is struggling to break even, you may find a commercial publisher willing to purchase it and even pay your association a continuing royalty for the rights to use the association's name and for distributing the publication to its membership list. Examine other products and services that may be of value to a for-profit business. Few associations own substantial physical assets, but you could find a buyer willing to pay cash for an association-owned building or automobile.

Devise a payment plan for your creditors. An association with a negative net worth usually is managing to stay alive by not paying its bills. Obviously, this is a short-term solution at best, because sooner or later, your suppliers will cut you off and may even haul you into court.

The National School Public Relations Association found itself with unpaid bills totaling $281,941 that was owed to 73 creditors. It proposed to its creditors a plan that it referred to as "an informal Chapter 11," whereby it promised to use a pay-as-you-go system for all essential current expenses and would repay the outstanding debt at a rate of 5 percent per month (or more, if it had it) until the debt was repaid. To maintain credibility with its creditors, it sent its creditors a copy of its current balance sheet along with the payment each month so creditors could monitor the progress. Not only did all the creditors go along with the plan, but the association received several letters of commendation for its forthrightness and its dedication to clearing up its debts. In

---

Turnaround Tip No. 16

"Get your Board aligned and working as one group. The best way to do that is to get them involved in the planning process."

—Janet B. Bray, CAE

Executive Vice President, National Association of Enrolled Agents

extreme cases, associations have been known to negotiate with suppliers a reduced amount in exchange for a promise to repay the balance. As New York real estate mogul Donald Trump has been quoted as saying: "If I owe the bank $1 million and am unable to repay it, then I have a problem; but if I owe the bank $100 million, the bank has a problem." Subtract a few zeros, and the same may be true of your association's relations with its major creditors.

Revamping the Infrastructure

A turnaround association is in desperate straits, with its fund balance either depleted or rapidly depleting. One could define a turnaround candidate as one in which the dues (or taxes or contributions) plus net revenues from operations are financially incapable of supporting the infrastructure of the organization. Or to put it another way: Because of a combination of internal and external factors, the organization can no longer afford to do all that it was once capable of doing to support its mission.

Until it puts its financial house in order, the association must either quit performing some unprofitable services (even though they may be desirable in terms of the mission) or it must reduce its staff and overhead.

Staff Reductions

The obvious way to reduce staff is to eliminate one or more positions, then spread the work around to the survivors and/or outsource a portion of the job. You may have to do this. But there are alternatives to reduce your staff expense.

Reduce work hours. As you've downsized the operation, certain jobs, such as data entry, will decline as well, so that what was once a fulltime job now can be converted to a part-time position. If you're lucky, the employee might be reaching a point in his or her life when shorter hours will be welcomed. Or perhaps an editor on your staff has always dreamed of a career as a freelancer. Your association could be that employee's first client. He or she could continue to produce your publication at a considerable savings in staff expense.

Reduce the salary. This is a tricky one, because you are asking an employee to continue doing the same amount and quality of work at a lower salary. I was once offered this "opportunity" after successfully downsizing an operation that reported to me. The downsized position, with fewer employees reporting to it, was now worth fewer "points" on the salary schedule. In that situation, I considered the offer an insult, and I quit. But an association in trouble might be more successful in convincing certain employees that their positions must be either downgraded in salary or eliminated altogether.

Early retirement. Several organizations have begun a downsizing operation by first providing incentives for older employees to retire early. This works better for large organizations that need to cut thousands of positions than it does for the typical trade association with fewer than twenty-five employees. Also, it could result in the loss of key employees that you'd like to keep. Nevertheless, it's an option that might be used in special situations.

Temporary furloughs. Just as some public schoolteachers are laid off for the summer, you might determine that some positions may be unnecessary for a few months and that the employees in those positions might agree to take unpaid leave until you're ready to staff up again.

Outsourcing

Whether you eliminate staff positions or reduce the amount of work you are paying your present staff to accomplish, you still must get the required work done. This often means outsourcing certain functions. The chief advantage of outsourcing is that you can obtain top-flight talent who can devote a portion of their time to your needs. You pay for this talent only when you need it; more important, you do not pay for this talent when you do not need it.

One misconception about outsourcing is that you are getting this talent without the need to pay for employee benefits. This is not true. You are still paying for the contractor's health insurance and vacations, because these items are worked into the contractor's fees. A talent that might cost you $20 an hour in salary for a fulltime employee probably will be charged to you at a fee approaching $30 an hour, because that fee must cover the expenses the contractor has to pay. The savings in outsourcing comes primarily from the fact that you are purchasing only a portion of the individual's time. The rapid growth in temporary employment firms is rooted in the fact that organizations today are hiring fulltime employees to handle the slack periods and supplementing that staff with temporary employees to accommodate peak periods.

Another phenomenon occurring that is due in large part to changing technology is that the best people in many fields are refusing to work fulltime for a single organization. Instead, they are striking out on their own as independent contractors as soon as they have developed sufficient expertise and confidence to do so. This applies to professionals such as editorial writers, advertising copy writers, speechwriters, newsletter editors, desktop publishers, typesetters, artists, photographers, meeting planners, travel agents, attorneys, and accountants, just to name a few. The implications are that if you want quality work by the best in the field, it may be necessary—as well as cost effective—to outsource.

Increasing Revenues

There are ways to increase revenues from existing sources.

Raise dues. This move strikes terror in the heart of many association executives and their volunteer leaders. I have been involved in several dues-increase situations where the prevailing assumption was that membership would decline significantly; yet I have never seen that happen. Most of your members are accustomed to seeing prices of everything they purchase increase on a regular basis, and your dues increase is likely to be met with a ho-hum reaction. Several executives interviewed for this book raised cash by increasing dues and enjoyed similar reactions. Before raising dues, you should compare your association's dues with those charged by other organizations within your member interest area. Resist the urge to assume that any dues increase will result in an offsetting failure of current members to renew.

The Treasury Management Association found that its dues were substantially below the average charged by similar associations. Donald E. Manger, its president, recommended to his board a 51 percent dues increase, and retention came in the following year at virtually the same level as before.

Reprice services. Just as associations are reluctant to raise dues, many are reluctant to increase fees for services performed for their members. Here again, a comparison with fees charged for similar services by other associations often will reveal instances where you are pricing below the prevailing level. The biggest payoffs often are experienced in conference fees and trade show exhibits. When you tell your members that implementing just one idea from a conference will pay for the registration fee many times over, don't think that your members have not already arrived at a similar conclusion.

Acquire sponsorships. Associations have tapped their vendor members for all kinds of sponsorships, ranging from refreshment breaks at conferences to special editions of the monthly newsletter. The Upstate New York Chapter of the International Association for Financial Planning found sponsors for each of its chapter meetings who were willing to pay for sponsorship on a sliding scale based on attendance. Chapter Administrator Nancy C. Carleton, CAE, explains how they did it:

"We told them they would pay $500 with a guarantee of 30 people. If attendance was fewer than 30, they got $100 back, plus $10 for every person fewer than 30. If we got 50 people, they paid us an extra $100, plus $10 a head for every person over.

"The sliding scale convinced sponsors that we were serious about delivering bodies for them to talk to. They get 15 minutes of podium time. After the meeting, we give them a printout of all the planners who attended the meeting."

As a result of the sponsorships, the chapter provides a meeting, complete with lunch, at no cost to its members. "We also encourage our members to bring a colleague who might be a potential member to the meeting," Carleton says, "and they can come free…. If they want to come back without joining, it costs them $30 a time for the continuing education, but we get a lot of new members that way."

7 | Communications Options

Communications is one of the key factors in a turnaround situation. Communications means different things to different organizations. Associations direct communications to four key publics: staff, top elected leaders, board of directors, and members.

Staff

No group understands the plight of the association better than its staff. As the frontline troops, they are the first to sense that membership isn't growing or that attendance is faltering or that book sales are slipping. Whether they fully understand the financial plight of the organization depends on how much the executive has told them.

The executive director, as leader of the staff, must be candid and open with them, because their careers are at stake. Often, the turnaround executive is new to the organization and needs to become acquainted with each member of the staff.

Gene Bergoffen, CAE, was particularly conscious of staff communications when he assumed staff leadership of the National Private Truck Council. Twice before, he had been a staff member in an association turnaround and felt that staff relations had been given short shrift. He was determined not to let that happen in his new assignment.

In the first two weeks on the job, he gave each staffer a questionnaire to fill out that gave him the essential information about the individual and his or her responsibilities. Then he scheduled a meeting with each staff member that not only provided insights about the person, but also helped Bergoffen understand the association's critical problems and opportunities.

In "Managing a Turnaround," an article he wrote for *Association Management* (December 1991), Bergoffen suggests that establishing task groups is a good way to evaluate staff abilities individually and in a team context. He put together an annual meeting planning team, a publications review group, an office equipment assessment group, an office automation team, and even a files identification and retention policy team.

These teams met during the "sizing up" stage of the turnaround, a period "characterized by high energy, a flurry of activity in many directions, a great deal of interaction, and a challenge to the effective use of personal and organizational time," Bergoffen says.

"I strongly recommend managers resist any inclination to restructure the organization at this stage," he warns. "It is a time for tolerance of ambiguity. Although many staff will be uncomfortable with this seeming disorder, you need the time to think through alternatives and to fully evaluate the abilities of staff. It may be helpful, however, to make small decisions that yield tangible results to demonstrate you're capable of decisive actions."

Another executive who took a strong proactive stance with staff at the onset of the turnaround process is Michael J. Naples,

---

> **Turnaround Tip No. 17**
>
> "To me, the whole turnaround thing revolves around doing whatever is necessary to find out how the members really feel, and what they really need, and then doing whatever can be done within reason to meet those needs."
>
> —**Nancy C. Carleton, CAE**
>
> President, Peripheral Services, Inc.

who was president of the Advertising Research Foundation in the 1980s. "My first act," Naples writes in *Association Management* (May 1985), "was to present a blank piece of paper to each department head, asking for a 10-year statistical history of the section. Financial information was important, but I also wanted other numbers: membership, advertising pages, volunteers, and so forth. When these sheets were returned to me, I became fully aware of the depth of the problem and urgency of our cash-flow bind."

With this beginning, Naples and his staff whipped together a strategic plan in two weeks, complete with 100 strategies and 300 tactics.

The chief staff officer of a seventy-person national organization in Chicago inherited a staff whose morale was perceived to be quite low, which is not uncommon in a turnaround situation. "We began to communicate honestly and regularly" with the staff, he says.

Monthly all-staff meetings were supplemented with a weekly letter from the executive to staff. His monthly communication to the volunteer leadership was distributed to staff as well.

"I developed a truly open-door policy for anyone who wanted to come in and talk," he says. "We communicated the idea that their jobs were valuable. We also raised the bar, indicating clearly that we expected people to work harder, longer, and better, and that we needed more performance. It was just a reality that the association had to get more work out the door if we were to be successful."

The Board and Its Leaders

Volunteer leaders are the next most critical public for the executive director to communicate with during a turnaround. Particularly important are the chief elected officer and the chief-elect, because they feel a personal responsibility for the continued existence of the organization.

Here, egos are important; it is the rare board chair who relishes the thought of the association going belly-up on his or her watch. Consequently, if the leaders have been kept in the dark about the association's financial situation by the previous management, the wake-up call of a crisis often arouses them to a frenzy that requires careful attention from the executive.

Next to being told that doomsday is right around the corner, the thing they fear most is an unpleasant financial surprise. That's why regular and honest communication with the leadership is critical. The danger is that the leadership will forsake its long-term visioning responsibilities and concentrate, instead, on micromanaging the day-to-day affairs of the association.

It is not uncommon for the chief executive officer to talk with the chief elected officer almost on a daily basis at the beginning of a turnaround operation. It is common for the two to engage in scheduled weekly conversations. Weekly telephone conference calls with the entire Executive Committee are also common and help to keep the leaders informed without unduly interfering with the staff director's day-to-day responsibilities of managing the headquarters.

The executive director should issue monthly written reports to the entire board of directors—even after the association comes out of the crisis. The monthly report should be sent out with updated financial statements, including the income statement and the balance sheet, with an explanation by the executive of significant variations from budget.

"Communication is everything," contends Ty E. Gable, CAE, of the National Precast Concrete Association. "And good financial information is a key. Not only accurate, but current. They should see the financials at least monthly, and the numbers should be current."

Stephen F. Mona, CAE, chief executive officer of the Golf Course Superintendents Association of America, goes a step further. He highlights key indicators at the front of the financial statements, including membership numbers and conference registrations, that serve to clarify the status of the association as of the beginning of each month of the year.

Perhaps the most important point to remember when communicating to the board is that the board expects the executive to have a plan for coping with the crisis. If the executive's report to the board says, in effect, that the association is going to hell in a hand-basket and that the executive doesn't know what to do about it, the board members' natural response will be, "Well let's get someone aboard who does." The gloom-and-doom report to the board should contain some expressions of hope and, certainly, suggestions for action. It is better to propose something that may be the wrong thing than to propose nothing at all.

The Members

Unlike a typical retail business establishment, an association is largely invisible to its members. The association exists primarily in the minds of its members, and this vision is shaped by the communications pieces received from the association.

The report you send to your board may be so well received that they may recommend you share it with the entire membership. That's what happened to Frederick D. Hunt, Jr., of the Society of Professional Benefit Administrators.

"In my first weeks," he says, "I started a candid memo/newsletter for the Board called 'Update.' It looked and was written much like the informal meaty Kiplinger letters. They liked the first issue so much that they said, 'this is the kind of information that all members need, so don't limit it just to us. Send it to everyone.'"

As a result, "Update" became a "private correspondence memo" sent just to members without a fixed publication schedule. "When there's news, we go to print," says Hunt. "Sometimes it's 20 issues in a year; sometimes 40."

It is a judgment call as to how much you tell the

membership about the association's financial troubles. Some executives argue that you should be completely candid and open. Jeffry W. Raynes, CAE, of American Production and Inventory Control Society said: "We couldn't generate enough information. We wanted to make it very clear what steps we were taking, and why, and what was surrounding those decisions and the implication of those decisions. If anything, we probably erred on the side of killing too many trees."

Michael T. Dunham believed in telling them as much as they want or need to know, but not volunteering too much. As executive vice president of the Northeastern Florida Chapter of Associated General Contractors of America, Dunham called on each of his forty-five general contractor members and responded to each, based on how much the member already knew. If the member indicated that he or she was aware of problems, but not the nature of those problems, Dunham would acknowledge that there were some problems but that steps were being taken to deal with them.

On the other hand, if a member indicated a real understanding of the depths of the problems, Dunham would respond with the full story. "Those that didn't have a clue," he says, "well you just didn't bring it (the crisis) up. You said we're going to do some positive things as an organization."

There are other situations in which members are completely unaware that the association has been experiencing problems. In those cases, most of the turnaround executives interviewed agreed that the executive should talk about the future and how the association will help its members deal with that future.

"You have to be candid, but you must be positive," contends Robert E. Becker, J.D., CAE, president of the Bostrom Corporation and a past president of the Chicago Society of Association Executives. "You cannot be a pessimist as your public posture. They (the members) have to have something to look forward to. It's okay to have your crises, and you have to have someplace to spill your guts about it, but it's not to your whole membership. You make that list of bad things minimal, and you make them truthful. And you don't exaggerate them. You have to be candid, but you don't have to focus on the negatives."

Ty E. Gable sums it up this way: "Image is everything. If members believe the association is second rate and no good, they vote with their dues check. But if you can get them to believe and understand that you're doing great things, moving ahead, aggressive and are helping them to succeed, then they'll stay with you."

The number of options in a turnaround is limited only by the imagination of the association's staff and volunteer leaders. In considering a few operations, program, financial, and communications options available to you, this book barely scratched the surface. However, the suggestions purposed here should persuade you to keep an open mind as well as an open ear for solutions.

> **Turnaround Tip No. 18**
>
> "Have a direction. People want to know that you have a definite sense of where you want to go."
>
> **—Donald E. Manger**
> President/CEO, Treasury Management Association

8 | Characteristics of Turnaround Managers

If only you could be told that "if you execute the following ten steps, you will be able to turn around any faltering association." Unfortunately, that is not possible. Association management is an art; it is not a science. Associations come in all shapes and sizes, representing every kind of special-interest group and coping with every imaginable external and internal event. Consequently, there is no cookie-cutter approach to curing them when they get sick.

However, there are certain patterns, attitudes, and attributes that are shared by many executives who have engineered a turnaround. These should be considered by anyone attempting an association turnaround.

1. They do whatever it takes to get the job done. They don't stand on formalities or job descriptions. They focus on the goal and work incessantly toward it, even when the actions they take are unpopular.

2. They combine a roll-up-the-sleeves attitude with a flair for the dramatic. They don't set out to steal the spotlight, but they are not afraid to make suggestions or to take actions that might attract attention.

3. They practice out-of-the-box thinking. They refuse to accept the answer that "it can't be done." They find a way.

4. They have a keen sense of the financial, but an even keener sense of human relationships. A turnaround is basically a financial problem, and they get to the bottom of it. But then they use their "people" skills to obtain buy-in for the solution, financial or otherwise.

5. Although they operate on many fronts at once, they establish priorities and patiently work their way down the list. In other words, they run a three-ring circus on a tight ship.

6. They turn lemons into lemonade. Turnaround executives are basically optimists, but they often are engineering the good breaks.

7. They communicate openly with the elected leadership, if not with the rank-and-file. They know when to spill their guts and tell it like it is, but they also know when to be diplomatic.

8. They practice the "vision thing" and keep their antennas finely tuned to changing member needs. They do formal needs assessment studies when they feel they have to, but usually their gut tells them accurately what it is the membership wants.

These are attributes any good association manager will possess, but in a turnaround situation, they become particularly useful and, in many cases, essential.

9 | Do Whatever It Takes

One of the reasons a turnaround manager often has a short career life expectancy with the organization in crisis is that he or she must be willing to do whatever it takes to turn the association around, even if it means stepping on some important toes.

Charles G. Ray, chief executive officer of the National Community Mental Healthcare Council, is one turnaround executive who has defied the odds. Ray came to his association in 1988 to turn it around, and a grateful board has kept him on ever since. Nevertheless, he feels that a true turnaround manager needs to assume that his or her tenure with the organization will be a short one.

"The board has to understand it's a short-term event," he says. "You need someone who can take a power saw to the organization. The change has to be made quickly. It's going to be dirty. It's going to be nasty. And that's when you bring in a terminator to come in and take it out."

Soon after he arrived, Ray slashed the staff, getting rid of "people who had retired but had not left yet," changed the name of the organization, established new categories of members, revamped the product structure, developed a strategic plan, upgraded the office computer system, instituted a member needs analysis survey, and challenged his staff and volunteers to think in terms of organizational cycles.

According to Ray, a turnaround executive must "have a passion; you have to have discipline; you must be able to motivate and engage boards who are anxious or worried."

An account executive with an association management firm contends that the executive director needs to step "into and out of the limelight as necessary, pushing board/volunteers up front to lead and get jobs done with less concern for board/staff turf, and focusing on the nuts-and-bolts of restoring the association's foundation."

After the early work has borne fruit, she cautions, "the executive director may find it difficult to change the behavior patterns established earlier. Once decision making is shared, or appears to be shared, between board and staff, people inside and outside the association may believe that the executive director is not a real leader, and he/she may have difficulty shedding the hands-on mode that worked during the turnaround. It is then important for the executive director to demonstrate his/her strategic leadership abilities in true partnership with the board."

Robert E. Becker, CAE, of the Bostrom Corporation, says that, as a turnaround manager, "your job is to be a change agent…your job is to take risks…and your job will only last three years."

Whether turnaround executives last a long time with the organization or a short time, many feel that the nature of their job is short-term, precisely because of the need to take unpopular actions to turn the organization around.

> **Turnaround Tip No. 19**
>
> "I owe so much to a Board of Directors that was willing to take risks, that was willing to give me the authority and was willing to trust me to do the things that they knew needed to be done."
>
> **—G. Martin Moeller, Jr.**
>
> Executive Director, Association of Collegiate Schools of Architecture

When Edward J. Collins attempted to make sense out of the files he had inherited at the American Economic Development Association, it was like putting the pieces of a Boeing 747 together after a midair collision. "Bit by bit, piece by piece, we unscrambled the puzzle and put the pieces back together," he said, "or if there wasn't a piece, I created a new piece."

He even drafted the services of his wife, initially as an unpaid volunteer. She answered the phones, which kept ringing even though the entire staff had been terminated as a result of moving the headquarters from Kansas City to Schiller Park, Illinois.

"We operated from day to day and literally from hour to hour," Collins recalls, "trying to get this organization back on its feet again and in a mode where it could provide some measure of membership service. It was dangerously close to dissolution."

Chris Mahaffey, of the Chicago Society of Association Executives, was the recipient of high-priced (but unpaid) talent in the form of his board members. They called themselves the "Chicago 10," and each day a board member would come to the office—every tenth day—to answer the phones, update the membership rolls, and basically do whatever was necessary to keep the society going until it could build back its financial reserves.

"A lot of this business is trial and error," says Mahaffey. He spent much of his time, especially at the beginning of his tenure, "learning what works and what doesn't work."

Having been previously involved in startup associations, James D. Maloney, Jr., CAE, executive director of the Regional Consortium for Technology and Information Exchange, found that he could be successful by adopting the mind-set of a startup.

"Assume you have a blank sheet of paper," he says. "If you were to start this thing now, knowing what you know now, how would this association have to operate, and to what would we have to pay attention and why?"

Cort Durocher, executive director of the American Institute of Aeronautics and Astronautics, introduced a whole new technological infrastructure to his association. He then discharged those employees who were unable to be trained to use the new technology.

"It sounds like a crass way to go about it," he says, "but it's a survivalist approach in my mind, where in order to compete in the nineties, you have to be lean, mean, and able to justify your value added or go out of business."

With limited resources and monumental challenges, association turnaround executives are pretty much in agreement that "whatever it takes" is a pretty good description of the job they are paid to do.

10 | A Flair for the Dramatic

Turnaround executives combine a roll-up-the-sleeves attitude with a flair for the dramatic—sometimes actions are taken that are showy, but necessary to dramatize a point.

Consider, for example, G. Martin Moeller, Jr. Moeller took over the Washington Chapter of the American Institute of Architects (AIA) on January 1, 1990, in the midst of an industry recession. Here was a venerable organization, more than a century old, that owned its building, which was literally falling apart because of poor maintenance and managerial neglect.

Because of the recession, many of the chapter's members were suffering financially, as was the chapter. On top of that, the chapter was slated to be host for AIA's national convention a year and a half later. Significant layoffs were announced at local architectural firms just before the January dues renewal period, and membership was suffering.

Moeller reasoned that he was going to have to take drastic steps that could not wait for the usual board and executive committee approvals if the organization was to survive. His first board meeting was looming on January 9, less than two weeks after his first day on the job.

To impress on the board that he was a man of action, Moeller vowed to make a difference in the physical appearance of the chapter headquarters. He "bribed some friends with beer and pizza" to come down over the weekend to clean up the place, apply a fresh coat of paint, and make needed repairs. He even brought in furniture from his home to fill in some empty spots.

When the board arrived for its meeting, the visual impact of the spruced-up headquarters had an immediate effect. It gave Moeller the credibility to go to the board and say, "You need to give me the authority to do a lot of things unilaterally and quickly, with the understanding that I will keep you informed." They unanimously granted him the authority he requested, primarily, he felt, as a result of the visual impact of the changes he had made.

Because individuals who serve on association boards are busy with their own activities at their own companies, it sometimes takes a jolt of drama for the executive director to get the point across that nontraditional actions need to be taken for the organization to survive.

Janet G. McCallen, CAE, did it by taking the International Association for Financial Planning board to its first visioning retreat at a Girl Scout Camp. "We were in a lodge, not tents," she hastens to say, "but it was a far cry from the luxury resorts the board was used to. It helped make the point that the organization had to change, or it would be out of existence."

At the National Community Mental Healthcare Council, CEO Charles G. Ray was engaged in a successful consulting practice when he was asked to help turn the organization around. To alleviate the council's cash crunch, Ray continued to consult, but turned his $1,800-a-day consulting revenue over to the council. "One of my visions is that the CEO ought to be a revenue generator," he says. His personal effort was a major factor in reversing the council's $81,000 deficit in 1988 to a positive level of $405,000 by 1995.

> **Turnaround Tip No. 20**
>
> "Don't be afraid to make downsizing changes. The membership expects it when finances are imperiled."
>
> **—Elissa Passiment**
> Executive Director, American Society for Clinical Laboratory Science

Several turnaround executives report that they delayed issuing themselves a paycheck for several weeks—or even months—because of their association's financial bind. Others personally typed the copy for their association's newsletter or similarly invested "sweat equity" to get their organization past a particularly difficult period.

"My wife will tell you that she pretty much didn't see much of me for that first year," said one.

Added another: "I realized it would be a very demanding job, and it was. Yet, over the seven years, it was both professionally and personally satisfying. I had no idea when I initially accepted the job of how close the organization was to failing. By the time I grasped the seriousness of the situation, I was beyond the point of no return. I just kept doggedly pushing ahead."

11 | Out-of-the-Box Thinking

One would think that "creativity" consultants would avoid clichés, but it seems that all of them begin their sessions with "out-of-the-box thinking" exercises. For those of you who have yet to be subjected to this exercise, it begins with the consultant drawing a box consisting of three rows of three dots each:

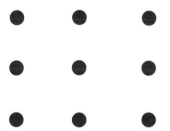

You are asked to connect all nine dots with four straight lines without lifting the pencil. The only way to do this is to allow some of the lines to extend beyond the boundaries of the box that is circumscribed by the nine dots. The creativity consultant then explains that thinking of possible solutions to problems often is restricted by a self-imposed box that limits the possibilities. You are then challenged to think outside of the box when confronting problems.

Successful turnaround managers are adept at finding solutions that defy conventional wisdom. They frequently come up with ideas that are outside of the box. Some of the options described earlier in this book, such as the bonds sold by David M. Patt for the Chicago Area Runners Association and the consulting that Charles G. Ray did to raise money for the National Community Mental Healthcare Council, fit the out-of-the-box description.

Sometimes volunteer leaders will surprise you with their own out-of-the-box solutions. Chris Mahaffey, of the Chicago Society of Association Executives, was initially turned off by President Ronald S. Moen's suggestion that the society sponsor a major trade show in December—in the midst of the holiday shopping season and in competition with similar industry events. But Mahaffey now credits Moen for persisting on establishing the annual event, which now generates more than one-fourth the annual revenue of the society.

In another example of out-of-the-box thinking, the past presidents of the National School Public Relations Association met and asked executive director Richard Bagin what they could do to help. Together, they came up with the association's Past Presidents Workshop. Since then, several workshops have been held, and they have proven to be a profitable venture for the association.

Out-of-the-box solutions will come at you when you least expect them. Richard L. Goodson, of the Iowa League of Saving Institutions, got the idea of forming a for-profit association management subsidiary with his existing staff when it was suggested by his counterpart from another Midwestern state. This colleague's offhand remark, said partly in jest ("I think I'll form an association management company"), became, in Goodson's fertile mind, an action agenda that saved his operation and launched him and his staff on an exciting journey into the future. Similarly, James A. Schuping made a "radical shift" in the National Computer Graphics Association by restructuring it as an umbrella organization that provides administrative services and marketing support for industry-related groups.

Occasionally, an executive will take an action that bets the farm (or at least a major part of it) and sets the tone for a rebound. Douglas E. Raymond, president and CEO, infused life into the annual conference of the Retail Advertising and Marketing Association International by increasing the audiovisual budget for the conference from $3,500 to $36,000 because he was dealing with advertising executives who are visually oriented. The gamble worked, with annual paid registrations growing from less than 400 in 1988 to more than 1,000 in 1996.

Raymond contends that a turnaround executive must be willing to take a risk. "You can't be squeamish about it," he says. "If you try to do it in baby steps, the organization is going to ground itself. You might as well just go for it, strategically thinking it through, of course, but go for it and hope that the chips will fall where they are supposed to fall."

Then there are the accidental, yet fortuitous, happenings. Frederick D. Hunt, Jr., of the Society of Professional Benefit Administrators (SPBA) makes a point of doing "whatever is the opposite of the orthodoxy of what most other associations do." He was emboldened by a potentially disastrous situation early in his career with SPBA. When he went to his first convention, he had assumed that the volunteer program committee had arranged for a convention program, complete with topics and speakers. The night before he left for the convention, he learned to his horror that the committee had expected Hunt to plan the program. He was heading toward a convention without speakers.

"Fate saved me," he says. "The convention city had a terrible fog, which meant our members were arriving in dribs and drabs at all hours. The chair turned to me and said, 'Since many of the people aren't here yet, do you mind if we forgo the sessions you

> **Turnaround Tip No. 21**
>
> "It is important to keep the membership proactively informed. You don't want to have member distrust or fear about where the association is going. There will be a tendency for members to place blame, but it all depends on how candid you are in your communication. There will always be some people who will not be happy no matter what you do."
>
> **—Laura Jungen**
>
> Account Executive, Smith, Bucklin & Associates, Inc.

had planned so we can just brainstorm about the good news and bad news we've seen in our business over the past year?'" The result was an open forum that was an instant hit.

"When I confessed the near disaster," Hunt recalls, "the board abolished the never-active Program Committee, and I was put in charge of planning all meetings from then on. We still have one or two Good News/Bad News Open Forums at every convention, and they're always evaluated highly."

Even at his spring meeting in Washington, where legislative and regulatory issues are discussed, Hunt defies conventional wisdom and refuses to book big-name Washington speakers. "Instead, we get the person buried in the bureaucracy who is actually in charge of shaping the regulation or legislation. Every member's ego would love to see a 'big name,' but I bluntly ask them whether ego or information is more important." His association also forgoes the issuance of formal position statements on legislative issues, preferring instead to be courted by proponents of both sides of controversial issues.

One may think that many of the examples cited here are representative of executives who were lucky rather than smart. But many executives have declared that if given the choice between being lucky or being smart, they'd choose luck every time.

But to be lucky, you have to start thinking outside of the box

12 The Human Factor

Make no mistake about it: A turnaround crisis is a financial crisis. Yet, the solutions are only partially financial. To a significant extent, they are grounded in the human relations aspect of the association. That is why successful turnaround executives have a keen sense of financial aspects and an even keener sense of human relationships.

The human relations side of the equation is important in associations because the individuals involved do not have a personal financial stake in the outcome. Contrast this with the for-profit organization that has several shareholders, including practically every member of the board, each of whom has plunked down a chunk of his or her hard-earned investment capital to purchase stock in the enterprise in hopes of earning financial dividends. They come at the problem with a common agenda: to make a profit.

Although it is true that the association staff have a financial stake in that the association is their employer, no staff member owns stock in the enterprise, nor can staff members anticipate receiving dividends.

Each of the board members, on the other hand, has his or her own agenda in serving as a volunteer leader. In many cases, that agenda is an altruistic one—to advance the mission of the association. But there are other agendas as well: Personal prestige within the industry, the company, and/or the community; free trips to exotic locations for board meetings; camaraderie with peers; a positive entry on the resume; and so forth.

The turnaround executive needs to be aware that the turnaround recipe must involve more than numbers on a financial statement. It also must take into account the nonfinancial needs of members and volunteer leaders.

An account executive with Smith, Bucklin & Associates, Inc., remembers walking away from her first board meeting and asking, "What have I done to myself?" Each board member, she found, had his or her own opinion of how the association should be run, based on their own experience with their own business. "What I tried to do in that first meeting," she says, "was to find as many of the board members individually and talk to them about their expectations. Other than surviving in their businesses and possessing a real passion for their association, I found they had few common goals."

Before beginning the turnaround process, Jonathan Perman spent his first few weeks as executive director of the Evanston, Illinois, Chamber of Commerce having lunch or breakfast with each of the twenty-nine members of the Chamber's board. Then, he had breakfast or lunch with each of the eighteen aldermen on the Evanston City Council. "I think I pretty quickly gained the confidence of the board and aldermen with my approach," he says. "The aldermen appreciated the fact that I wanted to bring the government and business together. If you give elected officers respect, you can get a lot more out of them."

David M. Patt, of the Chicago Area Runners Association (CARA), found that CARA's membership included several professionals, such as lawyers and financiers, who were willing to work for the association on a pro bono basis to help CARA rise above its problems.

"Very seldom do people say they belong to an association

because it has a great reputation for customer service or for the quality of its conferences," observes David E. Poisson of the Computer Dealers and Lessors Association. "It may be why people shop at a certain store or buy a particular car or choose to buy a home from a particular developer, but people tend to gravitate to organizations because of the affinities they have with others who belong to the organization."

Another executive noted that her association had a president who practiced an "imperial presidency." As she involved more volunteers in the decision-making process, the group developed a more collegial style of operation. This cultural change, she says, "is probably the most important thing in the long run that is going to make us able to sustain all of this."

Chris Mahaffey, of the Chicago Society of Association Executives, tells of one of his members who came into association management from the corporate world. This new association executive told him that in the for-profit sector, all the details of a proposal had to be worked out before presenting it to the CEO or the board, which then would give the go ahead to proceed. In the not-for-profit world, he discovered, the process was decidedly different. "It took this CEO a year to understand," Mahaffey recalls, "that in the volunteer sector you can't go too far ahead of the volunteers. If I were to come to the board with a brand new program completely worked out and ready to launch tomorrow, it would not work because there was no buy-in from them. In a volunteer setting, the psychology changes considerably. I'm not sure it is something that can be taught. It's learned. There's always this psychology of the volunteer governor who wants his fingerprints somewhere on any kind of a plan."

There's a tendency in a turnaround situation for the association executive to seek authority from volunteer leaders to take quick action without clearance from them. Some executives have been successful in getting that authority. But it is a risky strategy.

"Long term that style is not good for any organization," says John R. Waxman, president of the Sherwood Group, Inc., an association management firm, "because the volunteer leadership who needs to own this and make good decisions needs to be empowered, and they are never empowered with an autocrat at the helm. Initially, that might look good, but after that, if the leadership is not empowered in a collegial way, it won't work. A CEO needs to be a strategist, consensus-builder, and a collaborative partner."

One of the biggest human relations challenges stems from a board's tendency to micromanage the affairs of the association, especially if the deteriorating financial condition of the association was sprung on them as a surprise. The new CEO, hired to straighten out the association, often finds that the board is second-guessing every move he or she makes.

The directors of the Northeastern Florida Chapter of Associated General Contractors of America, Inc., had been so traumatized by the association's situation that its new executive vice president, Michael T. Dunham, found that every move was scrutinized by the volunteer leaders. "They questioned every paper clip purchase and wanted everything in triplicate," says Dunham.

"It was every bit of a year and a half before we could restore a level of trust with the board," he recalls. Dunham recommends that the executive document a benchmark at the outset to demonstrate "the good things that happened on your watch."

Perhaps the human element of the turnaround is best expressed by Donald E. Manger of the Treasury Management Association, who offers this advice: "Be consistent and ethical. People may resent your decisions, but will come to accept them in time when they see that your decisions are consistent, rendered with the interests of the organization foremost, and placing your own personal interest last."

13 | Operating on Many Fronts

An association under stress generally suffers on many fronts. A declining membership usually is accompanied by lower unit sales of products and services, which reduce both dues and nondues revenues. Smaller attendance at meetings translates into higher costs per registrant, because certain freebies thrown in by the hotels tend to disappear with a shrinking guest room pickup.

Nervous suppliers may demand payment up front if they sense either a real or imagined cash flow problem. Demoralized staff members take longer-than-normal lunch hours to interview for jobs at more stable organizations.

Tempers flare at board meetings as fingers of blame are pointed in various directions. The vendor community, picking up fewer new-business leads at the convention exhibit hall, may begin to spread the word to the general membership that the association is in trouble. To the harried executive director, it seems that troubles beget more troubles, and a true downward spiral takes hold.

Thus, the turnaround executive, who is facing problems with members, the board, vendors, staff, and creditors, must take action on many fronts simultaneously. By the same token, the executive needs to pick his or her targets carefully, because a sick organization can only stand so much change.

To handle the challenge successfully requires an executive who has a lot of energy, an optimistic nature, a stable personality, and a superb ability to plan and prioritize. Some executives think first and act later, while others act first and think later. The turnaround executive must think and act at the same time, often with a paucity of information.

The turnaround executive must stop the bleeding, reverse the cash flow, gather information, assess the staff's capabilities, write a short-term plan, set realistic objectives, generate fresh ideas, placate a number of angry people, and demonstrate to each of these groups that solid progress is being made—all in a seemingly orderly manner.

"We may have been too zealous, trying to accomplish too much in too little time," cautions David L. McMullen, executive director of the Florida Public Relations Association. "The result was several incidents where lack of planning detracted from the quality of the program."

Establishing priorities is critical and the priority list must be blessed by the executive committee and ultimately by the board. As John R. Waxman of the Sherwood Group puts it: "You must get the board to buy in to the realization that there is a problem, to get consensus on what the problem is and to get agreement on how we are going to solve the problem. The board has to buy into it or it's not going to happen."

Charles G. Ray of the National Community Mental Healthcare Council agrees. "In my mind, it was absolutely critical to get the board in agreement to sign off on a plan and to get it focused on its rightful purpose…vision and policy."

Ray cautions against fixating on one target. "Some people will go in and they will fixate on the board," he says, "or they fixate on the finances or on membership. You can't do that. You've got to be able to keep all those things moving or you're going to drop one. And that's why turnarounds are so tough. It's not that they're not doable, but they need a multichannel tending process that most people don't develop until they're in the crisis."

Waxman helps his boards prioritize by giving them three measuring points:

1. Does it serve the mission?
2. Does it meet members' needs?
3. Is it financially viable?

According to Waxman, the measuring points help board members to "focus and enables them to say yes to this and no to that, which makes our job a lot easier."

Robert E. Becker of the Bostrom Corp. says, "You have to prioritize services, and you have to drop services, and your board has to do that with you. You can't do that alone, for if you do, you'll be throwing out the wrong services."

Becker recommends that the executive be "ruthless" with the leadership core. "When you need a favor or need to be listened to," he says, "those thought leaders are there. But you do have to have the courage to push back. If you create an impression of leaderlessness or weakness or vulnerability or fear of loss of job, they'll smell it. And I don't think any of us, aggressive or unaggressive, is going to play that correctly every time."

Consultant Rodney S. Brutlag insists that a member needs assessment should be conducted before a list of priorities is established. "After the needs assessment and visioning," he says, "we have to ask, what are we going to do first? That creates a to-do list, and we can decide where we are going to start today."

At the Evanston Chamber of Commerce, Executive Director Jonathan Perman turned to locally based Northwestern University and enlisted a student group from the Kellogg Graduate School of Management to conduct a needs assessment. The assessment indicated that members of the

Chamber were interested in doing more good deeds for the community at large. "Using that [information]," he says, "we began to put together the pieces of an agenda for the organization."

Make sure you get the facts straight first before you act, cautions Mary Jane Kolar. "Your tendency is to change things as quickly as you can," she observes, "and in some situations you have to do that fairly quickly. But on the other hand, you can buy yourself additional grief by changing things you don't really understand. The tendency toward doing that is great, but resist until you have gained a basic understanding of what reality is."

An old hand at association management gave this advice to Janet G. McCallen, CAE, executive director of the International Association for Financial Planning: "If you've got problems on the staff and problems with governance, don't try to figure out which one you're going to deal with and put the other one off. You have to deal with both simultaneously. For if you ignore the operations and focus on the governance, the board will lose its confidence in turning over the operations to you. On the other hand, if you're focusing on operations and ignore the governance, and the governance structure is set up to meddle in operations, you're not going to be able to do in operations what you need to do. You've got to work on both of them simultaneously."

McCallen advises, however, that you still have to focus. In this respect, it is helpful to have a chief elected officer who can keep the board from overloading you and the staff with relatively low-priority jobs.

"So paradoxically," she concludes, "even though you have to do several things at once, the ability to focus is extremely important."

> **Turnaround Tip No. 22**
>
> "The keys to your success are staying close to the members, keeping expenses under control, and becoming an essential resource to the industry."
>
> **—Frederick D. Hunt, Jr.**
>
> President, Society of Professional Benefit Administrators

14 | Turning Lemons into Lemonade

Turnaround executives have a knack for turning lemons into lemonade. They use adversity to produce positive results. They use their poor financial situation as leverage in advancing the turnaround. And they eliminate or restructure activities or practices within the association that are hanging around through inertia, even though they no longer serve a useful purpose.

A savvy turnaround manager will use the association's poor financial situation to negotiate better terms from suppliers, to rally member support for a special assessment or dues increase, and to appeal to its membership for pro bono "in kind" assistance.

"Financial distress forces one to discipline," contends Charles G. Ray of the National Community Mental Healthcare Council, "and when a board has been excessive in any way, one thing that pulls it back quickly is finances." Thus, a financial crisis "can either be the death of the organization, or it can be a rebirthing experience."

Janet B. Bray learned the hard way that chaos can be an association executive's friend, if handled properly. And "chaos" is probably the best word to describe the situation she encountered when she

> **Turnaround Tip No. 23**
>
> "I instituted a sort of a fill-the-mailbox philosophy. We sent tons of stuff to the members all the time. When they started complaining they were getting too much mail, I figured I had it just about right. If there were a clipping that involved them, we would send it to them with a congratulatory note. Anything and everything we thought might be of interest to them, we just kept filling their mailbox."
>
> —**Ross P. Kinzler**
>
> Executive Director, Wisconsin Manufactured Housing Association

assumed the executive vice presidency of the National Association of Enrolled Agents. The association had been without a chief executive officer for several months by the time the Search Committee had selected Bray for the job. In 1994, she walked into a situation that resembled a summer beach house after an unchaperoned weekend fraternity party. The office was a mess, with "wall-to-wall boxes."

Financially, the fund balance was virtually depleted, and the association had lost $60,000 on a $1 million budget. There were no office policies and procedures. And the board was sullen, if not mutinous.

Bray set up internal office procedures and job descriptions. She established a personnel policy handbook. And, she rallied her staff to prepare for a move to new quarters.

"The move was a great way to create a spirit of teamwork," she says. "We listed tasks to be done and assigned responsibilities to staff members." She took the current president and president-elect to the American Society of Association Executive's CEO Symposium, which was instrumental in convincing the officers that the association ought to have a strategic plan.

"When you have chaos," Bray discovered, "it's easier to make change. When it's stable, change becomes very threatening. There was so much chaos that any change was okay, so I was able to go in and do a lot of things that I normally could not have."

Bray skillfully used the problems of the association to achieve positive changes that would have been difficult, if not impossible, to make if her association's situation had been different. She turned lemons into lemonade.

Similarly, when downsizing an association to correct a deteriorating financial situation, many of the older programs that have outlived their usefulness can mercifully be discontinued. Doing so forms a leaner organization that can be more responsive to the needs of the membership.

Associations need to be willing to reshape their traditional paradigms and eliminate ineffective programs to maintain their relevance in the new millennium. "Business as usual simply won't cut it," says James A. Schuping.

15 | Communications as a Turnaround Tool

The ability to communicate effectively is one of the most valuable attributes a turnaround manager can possess. Of particular importance is communication with volunteer leaders, who collectively often have different agendas.

Communication is a two-way street. It requires both a communicator and a communicatee. That is to say, communication is not just output (talking and writing), but it also is input (listening and reading). An effective turnaround executive is good at both.

Input

Good input skills can tell the executive:

- Why members belong to the organization.
- How they perceive the organization.
- How suppliers to the industry view the association.
- Which suppliers are willing to provide pro bono help.
- In which areas members need help.
- How your association compares with its competitors.
- Which services are held in highest regard.
- The relative effectiveness of various staff members.
- Which board members have creative ideas.
- Which members are outstanding candidates for leadership positions.

Input for effective turnaround management is obtained by visiting members, talking to members on the telephone, reading evaluations from users of association services, reading trade journals that serve the members' industry or profession, and using online services.

Visit members. As the president of the Financial Institutions Marketing Association, I made it a point to visit a member each month "in their native habitat." My entree into the members' personal world was a request to interview them for a "Member Spotlight" profile, which was a regular feature of the association's monthly newsletter.

There is no better way to comprehend your members' needs than to visit them in their offices. You can tell a lot by their surroundings: how they fit in the organizational hierarchy, what kind of staff (if any) they have, and what they actually do on the job (as opposed to the assumptions you make from their official title). One of the questions I routinely asked was, "What are you working on today?" That one question alone provided enormous insights into the problems members faced on a day-to-day basis. Another turnaround executive got a quick handle on his constituents by visiting chapters. When he arrived on the job, he discovered that his predecessors had required chapter presidents to fill out a form to determine if the chapter rated a visit by the chief executive officer. "I thought that was the most arrogant thing I had ever heard of," he says. "If they are kind enough to ask me to come, I will come." In his first year, the executive visited twenty-one chapters and found it to be "an incredible experience."

He recalls a chapter president who asked, "What are you

> **Turnaround Tip No. 24**
>
> "Taking on a serious management challenge like this is not for the faint of heart. If you're close to retirement, you'll probably make it, but other than that, you'd better start embracing some of this change."
>
> —**Cort Durocher**
>
> Executive Director, American Institute of Aeronautics & Astronautics

going to do for us this year?" His reply: "We're not going to do a lot for you this year because we don't have the money to do it, but if you'll hang in with me and give me a year or two to get our feet underneath us here, we are going to be the kind of organization you can be proud of." He felt this level of candor was an important element in creating the cooperative atmosphere that would help make his turnaround happen.

In another example, the National Computer Graphics Association (NCGA) was having problems with its trade show when James A. Schuping was appointed president/CEO. To better understand their concerns, he personally visited the CEOs of the "heavy hitter vendor companies" that exhibited at the show.

"The vendors were very frank," he recalls. "Many had already written NCGA off under enormous cost cutting themselves, were specializing within their own companies, and were cutting back on national shows." Attendance was declining. Key vendors were opting out in favor of more "application specific" regional trade shows, which were perceived as more relevant and beneficial. These visits paved the way for a complete restructuring of the association, to give more attention to segments of the industry that were growing and interested in NCGA's services.

Talk to members on the telephone. Some executives feel they can be more effective on the telephone than in face-to-face visits. Ross P. Kinzler, executive director of the Wisconsin Manufactured Housing Association, says he installed a toll-free 800 number at the association to encourage members to call when they have a problem.

"I do very little visiting my members in person," he says, "only because it's a weird philosophy of mine that the more time I spend out on the road visiting a member, the less time I'm spending serving all the members. So I'm not big on road shows. Today I probably talked to about 10 members. If I had been out in the field, I would have seen two or three. Several of the members I called I was able to substantially help with their business."

Calls to your industry supplier members can be particularly useful, because they frequently visit your regular members on sales calls and can give you some inside scoops about issues that concern them.

Read evaluations from users of association services. An effective turnaround executive builds in a feedback mechanism for every association activity, not just conference evaluations. In fact, complaints are a valuable resource for determining how to improve a product or service.

Read the trade journals that serve your members' industry or profession. A helpful resource to understanding the external environment in which your association operates is the leading trade magazine that covers your members' industry or profession. An additional benefit of reading the trade journal is the opportunity to call or write a member quoted in an article. It gives you an excuse to probe members on other issues that may affect the services your association provides them.

Use online services. By tuning in regularly to Internet discussion groups that cover topics relevant to your members, a turnaround executive can stay "in the know" on the daily gossip and chitchat involving association members. One useful service is the Executive News Service on CompuServe that electronically "clips" any item from the leading wire services, including corporate news releases, that contain key words you specify. Here, too, you will see your members quoted in articles that may never end up in print.

Output

Writing and speaking opportunities are excellent ways for you to assure members and other stakeholders that your association is in good hands. Some of the ways turnaround managers communicate with their members and other vital publics are through association periodicals, memos to the board, memos to staff, participation on radio talk shows, Internet web pages, and attendance at chapter meetings

Association periodicals. No other form of communication beats the regular newsletter or magazine, printed on paper and delivered by mail, for getting the association message across to its members. Frederick D. Hunt, Jr., of the Society of Professional Benefit Administrators credits his Kiplinger-style letter to members, called *Update*, for a sharp rise in membership. It is "so valued in the whole broader industry for its candor, useful information, and timeliness that we have literally been offered bribes as high as $10,000 for a sneak subscription," he says.

Turnaround executives invariably change the format of the association's principal publication to signal graphically that the association is under new management and that better times lay ahead.

Memos to the board. Directors often complain that they don't really know what is happening at headquarters. In a turnaround situation, frequent board memos, written with the utmost of candor, are a necessity. Although it is not always a good idea to hang out your dirty laundry in a communication to the full membership, it is almost always considered good policy to "tell it like it is" to the board.

At the outset of a turnaround operation, weekly or biweekly reports to the Executive Committee are common. The full board typically receives a monthly report, with a comprehensive financial statement accompanied by an explanation of variances from budget by the chief executive officer.

Memos to the staff. Depending on the nature of the turnaround and the size of the staff, some turnaround executives find it useful to copy the staff on the monthly reports

---

Turnaround Tip No. 25

"Sometimes you've just got to cut your losses."

—**Patrick E. Winters, CMP, CAE**

President and Chief Operating Officer, National Association of Credit Management, Chicago-Midwest

distributed to the board. Regular staff meetings also are an excellent venue for keeping staff updated on the progress of the turnaround.

Radio talk shows. An executive at the association management firm of Smith, Bucklin & Associates, Inc., finds radio talk shows to be a fun and low-cost way of getting his association's message across to a general audience. Executive director of both the Cremation Association of North America and the International Formalwear Association, Jack M. Springer is frequently on the telephone, broadcasting to audiences throughout the country about issues pertaining to one or the other of his associations. His most productive effort was to take a quarter-page ad in *Radio-TV Interview Report*, published by Bradley Media Publications in Landsdowne, Pennsylvania. He is also listed in the *Annual Yearbook of Experts, Authorities and Spokespersons*, published by Broadcast Interview Source in Washington, D.C. He recommends a catchy heading to create interest in the topic, such as "Cremation—It's a Hot Topic" or "Black Tie Doesn't Mean Blah Tie."

Internet home pages. The home page on the Internet is rapidly growing in popularity as a communications medium. The market is growing exponentially as more and more persons access the World Wide Web for information on virtually any topic imaginable. Also on the Internet are list serves—informal discussion groups on various topics. Chances are, there are one or more list serves on topics that relate to your membership.

Chapter meetings. If your organization has local chapters or special interest groups that meet regularly, you should use the meetings to keep members up to date on the changes going on in your association. How candid you are in discussing the "problems" of the association depends on how widely known those problems are among the membership. In any case, you should convey optimism that whatever problems you are experiencing, you and the board are addressing them in a positive way.

16 | THE VISION THING

In the beginning, associations were created to fulfill needs that, for one reason or another, were not being met by traditional, for-profit organizations. Those needs may have been caused by punitive laws or regulations, the absence of education and training programs for an industry, a desire for networking among people with a common interest, or any of a number of other reasons.

Over time, the association hired a staff, instituted programs and services, and developed a culture or tradition that defined the identity of the organization. Because of the dynamic nature of society, the needs of an association's constituency continually change, and a farsighted group modifies its program of work in response to these changes. In some cases, the changes themselves are a direct result of the association's efforts.

As long as changes are made in concert with the needs of its membership, the association thrives and survives. In the early years of this century, the pace of change was relatively slow. Most associations were able to keep up with these changes, even when change in programs was preceded by committees that met infrequently or that took their time to resolve contentious issues.

As the twentieth century drew to a close, however, the pace of change accelerated, and many institutions were saddled with cumbersome change-authorization procedures that hampered their ability to move quickly. Accordingly, strategic dislocations developed that launched a downward spiral in the condition of the associations.

The executives most effective in turning around associations practiced what former President George Bush referred to as the "vision thing," with mental antennas finely tuned to changing member needs.

Unfortunately, there is rarely time or money in a serious turnaround effort for the association to conduct a comprehensive needs assessment. Yet the successful turnaround executive has the knack for cutting through the static of day-to-day operations to focus on those unfulfilled needs and do something about them quickly, including deploying the people skills required to convince the board that changes are needed.

Consultant Rodney S. Brutlag contends that "to trust your gut" is a risky strategy for assessing member needs, even if time and money are at a premium. "Unless you find out what's happening," he says, "you'll never be able to take that first step." In Brutlag's view, upwards of 80 percent of what you learn from a formal needs assessment will be the same as what you intuitively know to be true. "It's that other 20 percent that will be most important to you," he says.

Sometimes, money can drive you to make the wrong decisions. Consider, for example, the National Community Mental Healthcare Association. CEO Charles G. Ray found that the organization he had inherited relied too heavily on federal grants. "They had some grants to produce things the federal government wanted, but not things that the members wanted," he says, "so they had a fundamental disconnect between the association and where the field was going."

To reconnect the association to its members, he insisted that each product the association sells contain an evaluation mechanism, coupled with a no-hassle return policy if the purchaser is dissatisfied for any reason. His publications manager, for example, telephones everyone who returns a product to determine why he or she returned it.

In the meantime, Ray focused his board's attention on a vision for moving the association through turbulent times. "A vision," he says, "should talk about our commitment, our competence, and our opportunities. I have our board looking at our vision statement at every meeting."

In a volatile industry, the association needs to engage in a series of rapid readjustments. The vision, then, acts as a "stabilizing anchor," in Ray's words, that keeps the organization on course. "You can be on the right track and do the right things and still get hit," he warns, "if the train is moving faster than you are. So I am very humble. I feel like I'm about two seconds away from whatever is back there behind me, and my whole organization feels that way. We really are convinced that if we are to be a shaker and a player that we have to be absolutely focused on what we're about. The thing that drives us is that vision."

Jeffry W. Raynes of the American Production and Inventory Control Society has a similar attitude: "We did needs assessments, we did focus groups, we did environmental scanning. We had meeting upon meeting doing strategic programming analysis and going through and saying, 'here's what we're doing now. Does this meet our vision for the future, or do we stop doing this and do something else?' It was…an interesting process."

Although most of the executives interviewed were positive about developing a vision for their association and reaffirming the organization's mission with the board, the "vision thing" did have its detractors as it is sometimes practiced. Robert E. Becker of the Bostrom Corporation, for example, characterized some visioning activities as a "board manipulation tool" that tended to justify pet projects of the staff or the chief elected officer.

"I don't think it will help a lean and mean group in a

changing environment," he says. "It exacerbates the situation where you can't turn around very fast. Executed improperly, there is a danger that the visioning takes the strategic planning process to the nth degree and dilutes it and defuses it, so you can't even tell, other than the vision, what's left for strategy."

In his view, the vision, to be effective and to represent true buy-in by volunteer leaders, must "bubble up" from the board, without undo influence by the paid executive. If the executive drafts a vision statement and presents it to the board for ratification, Becker feels there is a tendency for the board to approve it without engaging in the intellectual exercise that produces a visioning statement from scratch.

But how does an executive obtain a true picture of the board's vision without either presenting board members with a draft vision for them to edit or engaging in a time- and money-consuming exercise with the board? Rodney S. Brutlag, who has facilitated scores of visioning sessions with boards, recommends that the executive seek written input from board members and other "thought leaders" within the association before the visioning exercise.

By reviewing and summarizing these statements and discussing the results with the facilitator before the board meets, the visioning exercise can be condensed to a half-day or full-day session that can be useful in confirming the priority decisions contained in the executive's short-term turnaround plan.

Many turnaround executives relied on random calling of members to verify the formal research, as if they really needed to personify the reactions members were expressing on the questionnaires and evaluation forms. G. Martin Moeller, Jr.,

---

Turnaround Tip No. 26

"You have to identify what winning will mean. If you're successful, and they're successful, what will that mean? And what will it look like? You've got to get the board to talk about it, to articulate it, because they may have very different ideas about what that means."

—**Mary Jane Kolar, CAE**

President and CEO, The Alexandria Group, Inc.

made random calls to members of the Washington Chapter of the American Institute of Architects when he was its executive director. "In some cases I would talk to a member for as long as 90 minutes or two hours," he recalls. "That was one of my rules…that I would talk with them as long as they wanted to talk. I tended to do it at the end of the day, around 4:30 or 4:45, but if they really wanted to talk, I kept talking."

Moeller modified the randomness of his calls to the extent that he contacted one person from each of the major architectural firms in the Washington area— "sometimes a junior member of the firm, who would be surprised to receive a call from me." He found the calls to be "very valuable and they gave me a good sense of what the members thought the association ought to be doing."

As a result of his calls, the chapter developed a public relations and government affairs program that previously had not been considered but that a number of members identified to Moeller as programs they desired of the chapter.

Ross P. Kinzler of the Wisconsin Manufactured Housing Association conducted a series of random calls to members as a means of learning about the industry, because he had come to the organization from a school boards association.

A more formal version of random calling was conducted by Nancy C. Carleton among members of the Upstate New York Chapter of the International Association for Financial Planning. She and her staff developed a script to ensure the calls were appropriately focused, but "we discovered that once we began talking to people, they wanted to tell us things, so we kind of threw away the script after we asked the first couple of questions. We primed the pump and let them talk, and we learned a lot of things about the chapter and what members wanted."

One of the things she learned, which many other executives found to be true at their organizations and which was mentioned earlier in this book, was that there is a lack of consistency between the needs of board members and those of the rank-and-file membership. Carleton surmises that perhaps no board ever truly reflects the makeup of the membership of an organization, because its members are all actively involved, are usually near the peak of their careers, and generally have a plethora of industry connections with people much like themselves.

To serve the needs of the entire membership, Carleton says, "the board must understand the perspective of people who are not so well-connected, who do not have access to the same sources they may have, who are at the beginning of their careers, or who are facing challenges board members may never have faced."

Carleton concludes that mail surveys, however carefully designed, "cannot elicit the kind of information that can be gleaned from even a brief personal conversation. In a pinch, it means talking with the people who rarely or never come to meetings, finding out why they don't participate, and taking whatever corrective action is necessary to get them involved."

Whether they possess a certain "sixth sense" or rely on formal research methods, the ability to articulate the vision of its leaders and the needs of its members and to adjust the program of the association quickly to be responsive to those needs is a turnaround executive's key to success in reversing the fortunes of a failing organization.

17 | SOME PERSONAL THOUGHTS

When I began research for this book, my objective was to talk to as many turnaround executives as I could to determine not only how they did it, but how their successful experiences could be adapted by other association executives facing a turnaround. I did not think I would find a magic potion that would fix any turnaround situation, and I was right. But I did find patterns of successful strategies and tactics, and these form the basis for this book.

I interviewed many turnaround executives for this book. In this final chapter, I present a summary and tell you what I have learned from talking to these battle-hardened veterans. At the end of each executive's interview, I asked for his or her advice to other executives faced with a turnaround. Their answers are reflected in the Turnaround Tips featured throughout this book.

Now, here is my own advice to my fellow association executives about turning around the fortunes of a declining association.

Don't expect miracles. There really is no magic potion. Association management is still an art; it is not a science. The formula that works for one will not necessarily work for others. And when success does come, it usually comes in small, incremental amounts. Absent a cataclysmic event, such as Ross P. Kinzler's landmark judicial victory for manufactured housing in Wisconsin, your victories are likely to be small ones.

It is better to be a partner than a dictator. When an organization is facing oblivion, its governors are more likely than at any other time to grant dictatorial powers to a perceived savior. Don't fall into that trap. The most effective turnarounds are the result of a partnership between the chief executive officer and the chief elected officer. The word "buy-in" was frequently used by the turnaround executives interviewed. Your turnaround prescription must be "bought" by the association's board of directors and, ultimately, by the members.

It is important to do things right, but it is even more important to do the right things. This is one of the toughest of situations to deal with in a turnaround. An organization must have a reason to exist. If it had been created to solve a problem, and that problem has been solved, then either it needs to find a new problem to work on or it needs to go out of business. It may be doing everything right, but if it is not meeting members' needs, no amount of excellence, professionalism, or salesmanship will save it.

Unfortunately, the members of the board of directors are probably the last to recognize that the organization no longer serves a viable purpose, because it continues to serve a purpose for them, personally. The executive needs to probe beyond the board to determine the true needs of the membership. Some have an uncanny ability to do this intuitively. Some require a more formal needs assessment process. For most of us, however, it is a little of both. We have a pretty good feel for the members' needs, but we must constantly feed our "gut" with personal visits to our members and a thorough reading of the literature, especially the trade publications, pertaining to the changing nature of our members' common interest. And when we can afford it, we need to test our assumptions with a professional research vehicle from time to time.

Integrity is your most important product. Rotarians refer to it as "The Four-Way Test":

1. Is it the truth?
2. Is it fair to all concerned?
3. Will it build goodwill and better friendships?
4. Will it be beneficial to all concerned?

Successful turnaround executives also employ the four-way test. They treat everyone with respect, be they staff assistants, board members, vendors, creditors, or just plain members. In the end, integrity gets them through it.

Loyalty to the staff is both a virtue and a vice. Are you a staff member who reports to the board? Or are you a board member whose primary responsibility is to maximize the productivity of the staff? In a turnaround, you have to be more of the latter than the former. Your true allegiance must be to the members. That is tough to do, because you see staff every day, and they have become your friends. Often, we feel that it is us versus them, where "us" is the staff and "them" is the board. But a turnaround frequently requires sacrificing staff for the good of the membership. When that happens, the executive must be fair to the staff, but must be loyal to the board.

Members welcome change, even as staff and the volunteer leaders fear it. Boards and staffs often are frozen into inaction for fear of the members' reaction to change. The needs of the membership may suggest that the annual meeting ought to be switched from a Sunday-Wednesday pattern in the fall to a Friday-Saturday session in the spring, but it still takes a good deal of courage to change a long-held practice.

The easy answer is to "do what's right," but there is always the fear that members will perceive change as a sign of weakness. This fear generally is unfounded. More often than not, members look on change as a sign of progress. It is wise to do what the marketplace indicates you should do. Ironically, a turnaround association is in most need of change, at a time when it is least capable of handling change. The lesson here is that you must change, but you must do it carefully and professionally.

Creative ideas for turnaround solutions will continue to evolve long after this book turns yellow with age. We should definitely stay in touch, and the Internet is the logical place to do it. If you would like to join an electronic discussion group on turnaround management, please let me know. My e-mail address is cbartling@aol.com.

Good luck. And may all your turnarounds be happy ones.

REFERENCES

Bergoffen, Gene S. "Managing a Turnaround." *Association Management,* December 1991.

Bibeault, Donald B. *Corporate Turnaround—How Managers Turn Losers into Winners.* New York: McGraw-Hill Book Company, 1982.

Buck, Genevieve. "Business World Grows Impatient Waiting for Kmart Chief's Plan." *Chicago Tribune,* 14 January 1996.

———. "Slash-and-Shutter Approach Clears Ground for New Growth at Sears." *Chicago Tribune,* 14 January 1996.

Business International S.A. *Restructuring and Turnaround: Experiences in Corporate Renewal.* Geneva, Switzerland: Business International S.A., 1987.

Byrne, John A. "The Best & Worst Boards." *Business Week,* 25 November 1996.

Dalzell, Bruce C. "Turnaround Tips." *Association Management,* July 1992.

DiNapoli, Dominic, Sanford C. Sigoloff, and Robert F. Cushman. *Workouts and Turnarounds—The Handbook of Restructuring and Investing in Distressed Companies.* Homewood, Ill.: Richard D. Irwin, Inc., 1991.

Drucker, Peter F. "A Turnaround Primer." *The Wall Street Journal*, 2 February 1993.

Ettore, Barbara. "Turnaround Is Fair Play." *Management Review*, July 1995.

Finkin, Eugene F. "Using Cost Management Effectively in the Turnaround Process." *Journal of Business Strategies*, November/December 1992.

Glaser, Robert J. "World-Class Performance Through Work Flow Management." *Association Management*, October 1994.

Goldston, Mark R. *The Turnaround Prescription—Repositioning Troubled Companies.* New York: The Free Press, 1992.

Goodman, Stanley J. *How to Manage a Turnaround.* New York: The Free Press, 1982.

Heller, Robert. "Turnaround Tricks Are a Short-Term Solution for Firms." *Management Today*, June 1993.

Heppenheimer, T. A. "Rescue at Sea." *Audacity: The Magazine of Business Experience*, Fall 1995.

Imberman, Woodruff. "Turnaround Management: The Mission, the Methods." *Business Credit*, April 1992.

Kovener, Ronald R. "Managing Cash Flow." *Association Management*, February 1991.

Lewis, Fritz C., and Charles R. Chandler. "The Urge to Merge." *Association Management*, March 1993.

Lublin, Joann S., and Alex Markels. "How Three CEOs Achieved Fast Turnarounds." *The Wall Street Journal*, 21 July 1995.

McMillan, Edward J. "Diversified Revenues Spell Success." *Association Management*, February 1991.

McMullen, David L. "An Association Recovery—Retracing the Steps." *Association Management*, September 1983.

Nadler, Paul. "Wanted: Directors Who Work for the Stakeholders." *American Banker*, 26 September 1995.

Naples, Michael J. "Back in the Black." *Association Management*, May 1985.

Pearce, John A. II, and Keith Robbins. "Toward Improved Theory and Research on Business Turnaround." *Journal of Management*, Fall 1993.

Peters, Tom. "A Manifesto for Association Executives." *Association Management*, November 1993.

Reimann, Bernard C. "Corporate Strategies that Work." *Planning Review*, January/February 1992.

Richardson, Bill, Sonny Nwanko, and Susan Richardson. "Understanding the Causes of Business Failure Crises." *Management Decision* 32, No. 4, 1994.

Romano, Gerry. "Reshaping the Association." *Association Management*, October 1994.

Runci, Matthew A. "Back from the Brink." *Association Management*, April 1992.

Shore, David A. "The ACE Principle: A Winning Strategy." *Association Management*, September 1993.

Shore, Lys Ann. "The Turnaround." *Association Management*, May 1985.

Shuchman, Matthew L., and Jerry S. White. *The Art of the Turnaround.* New York: AMACOM, 1995.

Silver, David A. *When the Bottom Drops: How Any Business Can Survive and Thrive in the Coming Hard Times.* Rocklin, Calif.: Prima Publishing and Communications, 1988.

Sloma, Richard S. *The Turnaround Manager's Handbook.* New York: The Free Press, 1985.

Stevens, Mark. "Jump-Start a Faltering Business." **D&B Reports**, May/June 1992.

Stewart, John, Jr. *Managing a Successful Business Turnaround.* New York: American Management Associations, 1984.

Sullivan, Barbara. "Call This Turnaround Artist Rambo, Not Chainsaw." *Chicago Tribune*, 30 July 1995.

Turnaround Management Association. "Early Warning Signs of Business Failure." *1990 Directory of Members and Services.* Chicago: Turnaround Management Association, 1990.

Walk, Ann M. "How We Got Out of Debt." *Association Management*, June 1983.

Whitney, Kenneth. "Building Commitment into Strategic Plans." *Association Management*, September 1994.

Appendix A

Sample Plan for the First Eight Weeks in a Turnaround Operation

Although each turnaround is different, there are some common elements. The following is an outline of tasks to perform during the first eight weeks in a turnaround operation, leading up to a meeting of the board of directors. It assumes a staff size of about 10-15 persons, but can be adapted for smaller or larger staffs. You may use this guide to help you build your own detailed to-do list, adding and deleting steps as necessary to fit your unique situation.

Week One

☐ With chief elected officer, set a time and place for a meeting of the board of directors in about 60 days. Recommend an independent facilitator to conduct a visioning exercise with the board. Designate a regular time for a weekly telephone call between you and the chief elected officer.

- Call a general staff meeting, with the following agenda:
    - Introduce yourself; provide details of your background. Review status of the association, as you know it to be.

- Ask for a one-page description from each staff member about his or her duties and those projects he or she works on, to be given to you before the end of the week.
- Tell staff you will be scheduling a half-hour session with each person during Week Two.

☐ Pass around a sign-up sheet that enables each staff member (except for senior staff) to make his or her appointments with you.

- Announce the time and place for the board meeting, if known; tell staff you will be presenting a turnaround plan to the board at that time for its approval.
- Advise staff that you intend to include any downsizing, upsizing, or staff restructuring in that plan.
- Answer questions.

☐ Meet with senior staff managers, with the following agenda:

- Tell them you will be designating one of them to be the operations manager, whose responsibility it will be to keep the present operation running on schedule while the turnaround plan is being developed. Tell them that it is your intention that the operations manager, assuming acceptable performance, will be a key person in any restructuring that will occur as a result of the turnaround plan.
- Pass around a sign-up sheet to schedule a one-hour meeting before the end of the week with each senior staff member; at this meeting you will be discussing his or her duties and responsibilities and the projects he or she manages.
- On a flip chart, compile a list of products, services, and other association activities that are included in the

current budget and program of work of the association. Beside each item, place an A, B, or C, representing the staff's consensus of the importance of maintaining that item in a new program of work.

A = Absolutely must include.

B = Should include, if possible.

C = Could discontinue, if necessary.

- Set a time and place for a weekly meeting of the senior staff.
- Do "rounds" to ensure that each senior staff member has the opportunity to ask a question or to make a comment.

☐ Conduct a thorough review of the association's financial statements. Verify the assets. Decide on a date and format for a monthly financial statement for distribution to the board of directors.

☐ Conduct a thorough review of the membership records, and verify the accuracy of the membership numbers, reconciling expected dues income with actual dues income.

☐ Review the association's contractual commitments, especially those dealing with future meeting sites.

☐ Read the association's bylaws and identify desired changes.

☐ Review the following achievements for Week One:

- Arrangements have been made for a meeting of the board of directors, and the directors have been notified.
- The executive director has gained a comprehensive understanding of the association's current financial situation, including its contractual commitments.
- Membership numbers have been verified, and the executive director understands the mechanics of maintaining the membership database.

- The executive director has received a one-page memo from each staff member detailing his or her principal duties and responsibilities.
- The executive director has met individually with each member of the senior staff.
- Appointments have been made for the executive director to meet with other members of the staff during Week Two.
- The senior staff have developed a preliminary ranking of priorities of the association's products, services, and activities.
- Potential changes in the bylaws have been identified.

Week Two

- ☐ Call the chief elected officer and review progress to date. Fax him or her a copy of the senior staff's consensus on the priority of association programs and seek his or her input. Discuss problems with the bylaws, if any.
- ☐ Meet with senior staff. With their assistance, compile a list of the movers, shakers, and thinkers among the members, including up-and-comers and former officers. Also compile a list of members of the vendor community who are most concerned about the welfare of the association. Send a letter to each person on this list, plus members of the association's board of directors, asking each to send you a statement (not to exceed one page) of his or her vision of the association some 10 years from now.
- ☐ Begin individual consultations with staff members. In addition to talking with them about their individual responsibilities, ask each one who they would recommend among the senior staff for the operations manager position
- ☐ Make one call a day to a different board member to discuss the staff's consensus on program priorities.

- [ ] Make one call a day to a different mover-shaker-thinker among the membership to discuss program priorities. Include, from time to time, someone from your "concerned vendor" list.
- [ ] Review the following achievements for Week Two:
  - The executive director has reviewed with the chief elected officer the preliminary priority rankings of products, services, and activities. The chief elected officer also has been alerted to potential problems with the bylaws.
  - The executive director has met privately with each staff member.
  - The executive director has begun a calling program with directors and key members.
  - The executive director has made his or her choice for operations manager.

Week Three

- [ ] Call the chief elected officer and review progress to date. Discuss with him or her the person you would like to designate as the operations manager for the turnaround period.
- [ ] Select the operations manager, and advise that person of your choice.
- [ ] Conduct weekly meeting with the senior staff. Announce the appointment of the operations manager. Review with them the comments you have been receiving from nonstaff members concerning program priorities. Discuss their assumptions of the causes of the decline.
- [ ] Announce the beginning of the program analysis; during Week Four, you will meet with the product manager for each association program, discussing it from a qualitative standpoint. Schedule those meetings.

- ☐ Draft the first section of the turnaround plan, titled "Situation Analysis." Examine the current status of finances, membership, and program participation, and present your perception of the external and/or internal reason for the decline.
- ☐ Review the following achievements for Week Three:
  - The operations manager has been selected and briefed.
  - The Situation Analysis section of the turnaround plan has been drafted.
  - Program review sessions with the appropriate staff managers have been scheduled.
  - The executive director has continued his or her calling program with directors and key members.

Week Four

- ☐ Call the chief elected officer and review progress to date. Receive input on the Situation Analysis section of the turnaround plan.
- ☐ Conduct qualitative program review with the manager of each association product and service. Schedule follow-up meeting for Week Five to discuss quantitative aspects of each program entity.
- ☐ Conduct weekly meeting with senior staff. Review with them the draft of the Situation Analysis section of the turnaround plan. Discuss with them emergency actions required to "stop the bleeding" of the association's assets. Determine three to five objectives for inclusion in the turnaround plan, and brainstorm various strategies to help achieve each objective. Discuss the formation of staff task forces.
- ☐ Conduct monthly all-staff meeting. Announce the formation of special task forces that you are forming to dea

with specific turnaround issues.
- [ ] Draft the second section of the turnaround plan, titled "Emergency Actions," in which you describe actions you have already taken as well as future actions for which you are requesting the board's concurrence.

- [ ] Review the following achievements for Week Four:
    - Qualitative program reviews have been completed.
    - Quantitative program reviews have been scheduled.
    - Staff task forces have been formed.
    - The Emergency Actions section of the turnaround plan has been drafted.
    - Objectives and strategies for the turnaround plan have been discussed with senior staff.
    - The executive director has continued his/her calling program with directors and key members.

Week Five

- [ ] Call the chief elected officer and review progress to date. Receive input on the Emergency Actions section of the turnaround plan and on the objectives and strategies drafted by the senior staff.
- [ ] Conduct quantitative program review with the manager of each association product and service.
- [ ] Conduct weekly meeting with senior staff. Review with them the draft of the Emergency Actions section of the turnaround plan. Discuss broad parameters of the turnaround budget that will be presented to the board for its approval. Make assignments for preliminary detailed budgets for each activity and schedule meetings for Week Six on the budget.

- [ ] Draft third section of the turnaround plan, titled "Goals and Objectives."
- [ ] Review the following achievements for Week Five:
    - Quantitative program reviews have been completed.
    - The Goals and Objectives section of the turnaround plan has been drafted.
    - Senior staff have begun developing budget information.
    - The executive director has continued his/her calling program with directors and key members.

Week Six

- [ ] Call the chief elected officer and review progress to date. Receive input on the Goals and Objectives section of the turnaround plan. Receive approval of the board meeting agenda, including a half-day or full-day visioning exercise to be conducted by an independent facilitator.
- [ ] Review each program budget item with appropriate members of the senior staff.
- [ ] Conduct weekly meeting with senior staff. Review the budget, and discuss actions required to present an acceptable budget to the board of directors.
- [ ] Write the Programs and Services section of the turnaround plan, and draft a preliminary budget for review by the board of directors.
- [ ] Review the draft of the turnaround plan with the chief elected officer and the chief-elect.
- [ ] Send the advance mailing to the board of directors, with agenda and background material for its upcoming meeting. The mailing will include the draft of the turnaround plan and the preliminary budget.
- [ ] Review the following achievements for Week Six:

- The Programs and Services section of the turnaround plan has been drafted.
- A preliminary budget has been developed for review and discussion by the board of directors.
- The turnaround plan has been approved by the top two elected officers.
- The advance mailing has been sent to the board containing the turnaround plan and budget and other background material that will aid in its preparation for the upcoming board meeting.
- The executive director has continued his/her calling program with directors and key members.

Week Seven

☐ Call the chief elected officer and review progress to date.

☐ Conduct weekly meeting with senior staff. Review the agenda for the board meeting.

☐ Prepare board presentation, including appropriate handouts and visuals, on the turnaround plan.

☐ Review the following achievements for Week Seven:

- The executive director has prepared his/her board presentation on the turnaround plan.
- Visuals and handouts have been prepared for the board meeting.
- The executive director has continued his/her calling program with directors and key members.

Week Eight

☐ Call the chief elected officer and review progress to date.

- ☐ Conduct weekly meeting with senior staff. Hear progress reports from various staff task forces.
- ☐ Make last-minute preparations for the upcoming board meeting. Present to the facilitator a compilation and analysis of the vision statements proposed by volunteer leaders.
- ☐ Review the following achievements for Week Eight:
  - Final arrangements have been completed for the board meeting.
  - Staff task forces have made their initial progress reports.
  - The executive director has continued his/her calling program with directors and key members.

Appendix B

The Turnaround Team

The author gratefully acknowledges the contributions of scores of association executives and consultants who have been intimately involved in association turnaround operations and, more important, were willing to talk about them. Most of those listed below subjected themselves to in-depth interviews about their experiences, and many of them expanded on those interviews with additional written comments.

Others were identified by the interviewees as persons with extraordinary expertise in turnaround management, while still others were quoted in books and articles about their turnaround experiences. These are the real experts, who generously gave of their time and talents to make this book possible.

Adams, Normer, executive director, Georgia Association of Homes & Services for Children, Fayetteville, Georgia.
Albert, Roger C., treasurer and corporate controller, Smith, Bucklin & Associates, Inc., Chicago, Illinois.
Anderson, Glen R., account executive, Smith, Bucklin & Associates, Inc., Chicago, Illinois.
Anderson, Mark C., associate vice president, Division of Personal Membership Groups, American Hospital Association, Chicago, Illinois.

Bacak, Jr., Walter W., executive director, American Translators Association, Alexandria, Virginia.

Bagin, Richard, executive director, National School Public Relations Association, Arlington, Virginia.

Beam, Allen, account executive, Drohan Management Group, Reston, Virginia.

Becker, Bruce R., account executive, Bostrom Corporation, Chicago, Illinois.

Becker, Robert E., J.D., CAE, president, Bostrom Corporation, Chicago, Illinois.

Bell, Kathleen M., CAE, account executive, Smith, Bucklin & Associates, Inc., Chicago, Illinois.

Benson, Bruce, president, Fibre Box Association, Rolling Meadows, Illinois.

Bergoffen, Gene, CAE, president/CEO, National Private Truck Council, Alexandria, Virginia.

Borawski, Paul E., CAE, executive director, American Society for Quality Control, Milwaukee, Wisconsin.

Boyd, John W., executive vice president, Carolinas Electrical Contractors Association, Charlotte, North Carolina.

Bray, Janet B., CAE, executive vice president, National Association of Enrolled Agents, Gaithersburg, Maryland.

Brutlag, Rodney S., CAE, president, Brutlag & Associates, Chicago, Illinois.

Carleton, Nancy C., CAE, president, Peripheral Services, Inc., Rochester, New York.

Christopher, Gregory A., executive director, Society of Professional Journalists, Greencastle, Indiana.

Coerver, Harrison, president, Harrison Coerver & Associates, Fairway, Kansas.

Collins, Dorothy J., president, Organization Administrators, Inc., Deerfield, Illinois.

Collins, Edward J., vice president, Organization Administrators, Inc., Deerfield, Illinois.

Dakin, Kae, executive director, Leadership America, Alexandria, Virginia.

Davis, Nancy H., executive director, Turnaround Management Association, Chicago, Illinois.

Dunham, Michael T., executive vice president, Georgia Branch, Associated General Contractors of America, Inc., Atlanta, Georgia.

Durocher, Cort, executive director, American Institute of Aeronautics & Astronautics, Reston, Virginia.

Fuller, Jerry, executive director, Associated Colleges of Illinois, Chicago, Illinois.

Gable, Ty E., CAE, president, National Precast Concrete Association, Indianapolis, Indiana.

Galvin, Roger A., CEO, National Spa and Pool Institute, Alexandria, Virginia.

Goodson, Richard L., president, Diversified Management Services, Des Moines, Iowa.

Graham, John H. IV, CEO, American Diabetes Association, Alexandria, Virginia.

Hacke, Kevin, account executive, The Sherwood Group, Inc., Northbrook, Illinois.

Hansen, Christine, executive director, Interstate Oil and Gas Compact Commission, Oklahoma City, Oklahoma.

Healy, John J., CAE, executive vice president/CEO, National Wooden Pallet & Container Association, Arlington, Virginia.

Holding, Robert L., president, Association of Home Appliance Manufacturers, Chicago, Illinois.

Hunt, Jr., Frederick D., president, Society of Professional Benefit Administrators, Chevy Chase, Maryland.

Jorgensen, Dennis, chief operating officer, American Marketing Association, Chicago, Illinois.

Jungen, Laura, account executive, Smith, Bucklin & Associates, Inc., Chicago, Illinois.

Kinzler, Ross P., executive director, Wisconsin Manufactured Housing Association, Madison, Wisconsin.

Knight, Mark A., executive director, American Association for Partial Hospitalization, Alexandria, Virginia.

Koblish, Bruce, president, Gospel Music Association, Nashville, Tennessee.
Kolar, Mary Jane, CAE, president and CEO, The Alexandria Group Inc., Alexandria, Virginia.
Kuehl, Philip G., consultant, Westat Inc., Rockville, Maryland.
Lesser, Philip, Ph.D., CAE, account executive, Bostrom Corporation, Chicago, Illinois.
Mahaffey, J. Chris, CAE, executive director, Chicago Society of Association Executives, Chicago, Illinois.
Maloney, Jr., James D., CAE, executive director, Regional Consortium for Technology and Information Exchange, Kansas City, Missouri.
Manger, Donald E., president/CEO, Treasury Management Association, Bethesda, Maryland.
McCallen, Janet G., CAE, executive director, International Association for Financial Planning, Atlanta, Georgia.
Moeller, Jr., G. Martin, executive director, Association of Collegiate Schools of Architecture, Washington, DC.
Mona, Stephen F., CEO, CAE, Golf Course Superintendents Association of America, Lawrence, Kansas.
Myers, Marsha, executive director, Gold Coast Builders Association, Boynton Beach, Florida.
Noone, Stephen J., CAE, executive director, American Academy of Osteopathy, Indianapolis, Indiana.
Passiment, Elissa, executive director, American Society for Clinical Laboratory Science, Bethesda, Maryland.
Patt, David M., CAE, executive director, Chicago Area Runners Association, Chicago, Illinois.
Perman, Jonathan, executive director, Evanston Chamber of Commerce, Evanston, Illinois.
Poisson, David E., CAE, account executive, Smith, Bucklin & Associates, Inc., Washington, DC.
Poyser, Tracy, account executive, Smith, Bucklin & Associates, Inc., Chicago, Illinois.
Ray, Charles G., CEO, National Community Mental Healthcare Council, Rockville, Maryland.

Raymond, Douglas E., president/CEO, Retail Advertising and Marketing Association International, Chicago, Illinois.

Raynes, Jeffry W., CAE, executive director and chief operating officer, American Production & Inventory Control Society, Falls Church, Virginia.

Runci, Matthew A., president, Jewelers of America Inc., New York, New York.

Samson, Joseph, account executive, The Sherwood Group, Northbrook, Illinois.

Schuping, James A., CAE, president, American Alliance of Family Business, Philadelphia, Pennsylvania.

Sherwood, Larry, executive director, American Solar Energy Society, Boulder, Colorado.

Soyars, Glenda, president, Florida Employers Exchange Inc., Sarasota, Florida.

Springer, Jack M., account executive, Smith, Bucklin & Associates, Inc., Chicago, Illinois.

Strandquist, John H., CAE, president/CEO, American Association of Motor Vehicle Administrators, Arlington, Virginia.

Tecker, Glenn H., CEO, Tecker Consultants, Trenton, New Jersey.

Trachtenberg, Robert L., executive director, American Psychiatric Association, Washington, DC.

Waxman, John R., president, The Sherwood Group, Inc., Northbrook, Illinois.

West, Dean A., account manager, Bostrom Corporation, Chicago, Illinois.

Williams, Raymond M., Ph.D., CAE, executive vice president, United Association of Equipment Leasing, Oakland, California.

Winters, Patrick E., CMP, CAE, president and chief operating officer, National Association of Credit Management/Chicago-Midwest, Park Ridge, Illinois.

Wood, Gale S., CAE, executive director, Financial Women International, Arlington, Virginia.

About the Author

Charles E. Bartling, CAE, developed skills as a turnaround manager as executive vice president of the American Society of Business Press Editors and as president of the Financial Institutions Marketing Association.

For 14 years, he served in various capacities with the Bank Marketing Association, including director of communications, vice president and director of education and information services, and corporate secretary. He was also an account executive with Smith, Bucklin & Associates, Inc., in Chicago.

He is a long-time member of the American Society of Association Executives and the Chicago Society of Association Executives. He is a Rotarian and a member of Toastmasters International.

A native of DeLand, Florida, he has a Bachelor of Arts degree in Education from the University of Florida and a Master of Science degree in Journalism from Northwestern University. He taught Principles of Association Management in the MBA program at DePaul University in Chicago.

He lives with his wife, Ann, an interior designer, in Evanston, Illinois.